Your Survival™

Any Disaster. Every Family.
ALL THE ANSWERS.

Your Seven-Step Plan for Survival ... and Peace of Mind:

1. Open up the sleeve at left, take out the enclosed disc, and pop it in your DVD player or computer. Look for your membership number. Write it down.

2. Go to **yoursurvival.com**, your new disaster-readiness headquarters. Type your membership number in the prompt box. Soon you will be able to store your vital documents on our high-security server, accessible from anywhere if your computer hard drive goes down. You'll also be able to establish a virtual family meeting spot, exchange ideas with experts and other members, and sign up for our early-warning service and a host of other privileges.

3. Start going through this incredibly practical, surprising, and entertaining 160-page handbook. Before, during, or after, watch the DVD for more insight and analysis, not to mention gripping storm footage and hard lessons learned.

4. Pull out the Your Survival Express Planner card at the back. Fill out the contact, account, and medical information in the spaces provided and tear off the shopping lists for Step No. 5.

5. Set aside part of one weekend for carrying out your marching orders: stocking up on supplies like hurricane lamps and "bug-out" bags, getting your other important documents together, vetting your insurance policy, going over escape routes, etc. Make it a family project. It can be fun! (Well, aside from the insurance part.)

6. Keep an eye on Your Survival™List, **yoursurvival.com**'s own bulletin board of disaster recovery resources for communities in crisis.

7. Never worry about a disaster again.

Your Survival, LLC

Text and DVD Copyright © 2006 by YourSurvival, LLC

HatherleighPress

5-22 46th Avenue, Suite 200
Long Island City, NY 11101
www.hatherleighpress.com

Library of Congress Cataloging-in-Publication Data
Arnot, Robert Burns.
  Your survival : the complete resource for disaster planning and recovery / by Bob Arnot and Mark Cohen.
     p. cm.
  Includes a one month subscription to www.yoursurvival.com.
  ISBN 978-1-57826-262-5
  1. Emergency management. 2. Survival skills. 3. Preparedness. I. Cohen, Mark, 1962- II. Title.
  HV551.2.A76 2007
  613.6'9–dc22

                              2007017407

Your Survival is available for bulk purchases, special promotions, and premiums. For information on reselling and special purchase opportunities, please call 1-800-528-2550 and ask for the Special Sales Manager.

For more information go to <u>yoursurvival.com</u>.

Art Director: Deborah Miller
Cover & book design by Christopher Hercik
Production Assistant: Allison Furrer

10 9 8 7 6 5 4 3 2 1

PRINTED IN CHINA

To all the victims and their loved ones who have recovered
– or are still recovering –
from this country's natural and manmade disasters

The Complete Resource for Disaster Planning and Recovery

Dr. Bob Arnot and Mark Cohen

HatherleighPress

New York • London

ACKNOWLEDGEMENTS

OUR DEEPEST THANKS go out to all those who generously gave of their time, wisdom, and hard-won lessons so that others could be prepared. First, to Ralph Swisher at the Federal Emergency Management Agency, who has forgotten more about disaster preparedness than most people will ever know. Nearly every expert source cited in this resource can be traced in one form or another back to Ralph.

Also, the American Institute of Certified Public Accountants, for granting us access to the organization's 340,000 members and their phenomenal roster of disaster-stricken clients. And special thanks to AICPA members Ken Strauss, Ken Abney, and Mitchell Freedman.

To Kathleen Tierney of the University of Colorado's Natural Hazards Center; Mike Lindell of the Texas A&M Hazard Reduction and Recovery Center; the Institute for Business & Home Safety's Tim Reinhold; Massachusetts General Hospital trauma surgeon Dr. Susan Briggs; University of Minnesota epidemiologist Mike Osterholm; Atlanta physician Dr. Grattan Woodson; University of South Carolina geography professor Susan Cutter; California Institute of Technology seismologist Tom Heaton; the U.S. Geological Survey's Paula Gori, Lucy Jones, David Applegate, and Susan Hough; Joe Schaefer of the Storm Prediction Center, Kevin Kelleher of the National Severe Storms Laboratory, and the National Hurricane Center's Max Mayfield and Ed Rappaport; Mitretek telecom specialist Gil Miller; Insurance Information Institute spokesperson Jeanne Salvatore; the Florida Disaster Contractors Network's Douglas Buck; Cliff Vaughn of Ground Zero Tornado Shelters; John Fitzpatrick of Centex Homes; Craig Delisle of Sunland Homes; Maine mental health specialist Christine Curci; and Baltimore insurance agent Jonas Cohen. If anyone ever establishes a "Disaster Preparedness University," they should hire these folks as the faculty.

To "Captain" Dave Reeder, or as we know him, "The Most Prepared Man in America."

To the survivors of our nation's disasters who shared their stories with us: Kathy Hebert, Pat and Susan Jordan, Joey Difatta, Todd and Karen Goolsby, Stacy Stice, Roberta Winston, Deborah Irabor, Joe Gallodoro, Christi Covington, Randy Thurman, Tripp Meister, Jill Lockhart, Tim Donohoe, Marty Francis, Mike and Stacey Yuja, the Barklow family, and Diane Stevens. Your honesty and strength is a source of inspiration we won't soon forget.

Last and most important, thanks to Sam Brown, whose energy and vision carried this project from start to finish, and to his able partner, Linda Daniels, whose enthusiasm and encouragement was a great benefit to the entire team.

CONTENTS

CONTENTS

CONTENTS

FOREWORD

OVER THE LAST 30 years as a physician and TV correspondent, I've traveled to dozens of the world's worst disasters. I've reported on horrific terrorist bombings in Jerusalem, helped with the relief efforts after city-leveling earthquakes in Turkey, and canvassed the war- and famine-ravaged African continent lending a hand to organizations like Save the Children. After each of these trips, I would return home to New York City, and as my cab sped down the FDR Drive, I felt a profound sense of relief and gratitude. But inevitably a thought would nag me: Why couldn't it happen here? What's different about us that makes us immune to tragedy on such an epic scale?

"The 9/11 terrorist attacks and Hurricane Katrina were a wake-up call for me, as I suspect they were for a lot of Americans."

The 9/11 terrorist attacks and Hurricane Katrina were a wake-up call for me, as I suspect they were for a lot of Americans. It turned out we hadn't been different or immune—just lucky. Massive explosions could, indeed, rock our major cities. Natural calamities could displace hundreds of thousands of our citizens from their homes.

If anything, these disasters showed that we're probably less prepared than many countries overseas. People in New Orleans died in their own homes from lack of the most basic supplies. For want of a simple communication plan, family members were bused to different cities and separated for weeks. Because of inadequate insurance and government coordination, huge swaths of the region remain as desolate today as they were in the days immediately after the floodwaters receded.

Twelve months ago, I got a call from a dear friend, Sam Brown. Sam had friends in New Orleans who'd lost nearly everything they owned to Katrina. These were intelligent people with plenty of wherewithal who were now living out of suitcases and battling with their insurance companies because they had failed to take even the simplest steps to plan for the unexpected. Sam figured if people like his friends could be so unprepared, there clearly was a need for more and better advice, and asked if I would help him do something about it.

Photo courtesy of hurricanecity.com

Your Survival™ is the product of that original conversation. A talented and dedicated crew of people has devoted thousands of man-hours to the project since then. Their sources included dozens of survivors and the nation's leading disaster authorities. I thought I had read everything there was to know about disasters—and I was amazed at what our team came up with. The vision, though, remains the same as the first time Sam and I spoke: We're not different. We're not immune. We're just like people around the rest of the world. And we need to be prepared.

—Dr. Bob Arnot

INTRODUCTION

YOU NEVER THINK a disaster will happen to you. Kathy Hebert, a 46-year-old physician and public health analyst certainly didn't. The longtime New Orleans resident always thought that keeping supplies and extra cash on hand, making copies of vital records, and buying supplemental insurance for rare events like earthquakes or floods were things that only "worrywarts" did.

Then Hurricane Katrina hit. Now, almost two years after the disaster, Hebert and her husband are camping out with a toaster on the second floor of what used to be their house. The first floor, which was inundated by five feet of water from the 17th Street Canal, had to be taken down clear to the studs; Hebert spends hours each week searching for a contractor who's not too busy to put up walls—which for now the Heberts must pay for out of their own savings.

"When the order came to evacuate we only had a couple of hours to get out," she recalls. "We had two big plastic totes stuffed with our important papers and other valuables, like our wedding video, and we put them up on our kitchen counters. So we figured at least those things would stay dry. Unfortunately, we

didn't count on the fact that, in five feet of water, plastic totes slide off counters and topple open! That was really hard. My father died nine years ago, and that was the only video I had of him. Now I just want to grab people by the neck and tell them, 'Don't put your faith in plastic totes!' You have to make sure stuff like that is in order and in one place so you can take it with you."

Kathy's story is exactly the point of the *Your Survival™* disaster planning, response, and recovery program. You might call it our attempt to "grab you by the neck" (in the nicest possible way of course), to get you thinking about all the things that thousands of people never do. To help, we enlisted the country's leading disaster preparedness experts, including emergency management officials, weather forecasters, physicians, engineers, accountants, insurance analysts, and grief counselors. We also interviewed dozens of survivors from all across the country. Smart, hard-working people just like you, who are still drying out from Hurricane Katrina and the 2006 flooding in the Northeast, people who have watched their houses slide down cliffs during earthquakes in Los Angeles, run from wildfires in San Diego, and cowered inside closets as F5 tornadoes ripped apart their Oklahoma homes. They all agreed to tell their stories because they have some hard lessons to share, and

"People think Bruce Willis is going to jump out of a tank, and suddenly all these supplies will pour in."

because they understand two important truths about disasters: First, these catastrophes can, and do, happen to anyone, regardless of income or geography. Second, at a time when it's increasingly clear that government is overmatched by the cost and coordination of recovery efforts, it's a big mistake to count on someone else to take care of these issues for you.

"A lot of people in this country have this idea that Bruce Willis is going to jump out of a tank, and suddenly all these supplies are going to start pouring in to help them put their lives back together," says Hebert. "Well, it doesn't exist. It's a fantasy that only lives in Hollywood. When something like this happens, every family better have it together and know how to take responsibility for themselves."

We're not trying to scare you with statements like these or get you to take up residence with your spouse and children in a bunker somewhere with a two-year supply of Meals Ready to Eat (MREs). We just think it makes sense to do a little advance planning now that can save you plenty of stress and heartache later.

Disasters don't need to devastate your family. Especially not if you have the right type of insurance, organize your most vital possessions, and prep with the rest of the quick and easy info outlined in *Your Survival™*.

ABOUT THIS GUIDE

YOUR SURVIVAL™ is a guide to your family's security. Like a good car or computer manual, it's designed to be as comprehensive and as succinct as possible. We've attempted to cover all aspects of disaster preparedness, from mundane reminders about stocking a non-electric can opener and extra doses of medications to the ins and outs of claiming damages as a tax deduction. But we've organized the material so you can quickly access the parts you need when you need them most.

As you and your family initially go through the guide and accompanying DVD, we suggest you focus the majority of your energy on the chapters in Part I: "Identifying Your Risks" and "Planning Ahead." Then familiarize yourself with

the issues raised in Parts II and III: "Stay or Go?"; "Weathering the Storm"; "Immediate Aftermath"; and "Rebuilding." And then store this guide with the rest of your vital supplies so you'll know exactly where to find it if you need an emergency refresher.

As you read *Your Survival™*, you may notice that some of our advice contradicts what you may have heard before. We were hoping that would be the case. The best disaster preparedness recommendations are fluid and always changing. Every major disaster that strikes this country contains valuable lessons on how to cope with the next one, and we've made a concerted effort to bring you the very best up-to-the-minute information—and with a depth and objectivity we don't think you'll find in the raft of free, publicly available advice on the topic. As helpful as FEMA.org and the Insurance Information Institute website can be for specific resources, they're never going to tell you how to cut through government red tape or win an argument with your claims adjustor. But *Your Survival™* will.

YOURSURVIVAL.COM

IN **ADDITION** to this guide, the DVD, and the Your Survival™ Express Planner checklist that comes packaged with it, there's another key element of *Your Survival™*. It's our website, yoursurvival.com, which we hope you'll soon start thinking of as your "disaster readiness headquarters."

As soon as you get the chance, we suggest you check it out. Each day, the site and its blog will brief you on all the latest, most pertinent headlines, bulletins, and storm-tracking info from Washington, DC, forecasting centers, and other key fronts in the disaster world. It will also include exclusive interviews with survival experts and real-life stories from people who have lived through a disaster in your area.

Log in with the membership code you'll find on your DVD, and you'll have access to:

• *a virtual meeting place where separated family members can check on each other's whereabouts in case of an evacuation or other emergency*

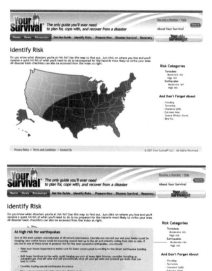

• *customized weather, disaster, terror, or other alarms, which may be able to ring to cell phone, your laptop, or Blackberry®, every time forecasters, the Department of Homeland Security, or local emergency managers issue an alert for your area*

• *step-by-step tutorials on how to disaster-proof your house to protect against earthquakes, floods, and fires*

• *interactive maps to help you assess what dangers you might encounter where you live*

• *a bulletin board where you can exchange ideas with other Your Survival™ members*

• a member dashboard including tools and checklists you can use to track your readiness status and remind you when you need to review or update your "bug-out" bag

• recommendations and links to the best publicly available resources for every disaster, including the National Hurricane Service, the Federal Emergency Management Agency, the American Red Cross, and much more

Soon, you will also be able to store your family's vital financial and health records on our state-of-the-art, high-security server, and quickly retrieve them from any Internet connection if your home hard drive is destroyed.

With the most up-to-date news on how to get ready for any kind of disaster, <u>yoursurvival.com</u> is an indispensable tool in your arsenal of preparedness tools. Keep an eye on the site for new features and news.

YOUR SURVIVAL™ LIST

On **YOURSURVIVAL.COM**, you will find an online bulletin board for communities struck by disaster. Whenever a major castrophe looms, Your Survival™List will spring into action with a blast of data lifelines, including lost-and-found and classified message boards, location-specific weather alerts, focused preparedness and response advisories, and community-generated updates about evacuation routes, response center locations, health warnings, relief backlogs—essentially anything that anyone directly affected by the crisis needs to know. Just go to the Your Survival™List section at yoursurvival.com— and pass the word.

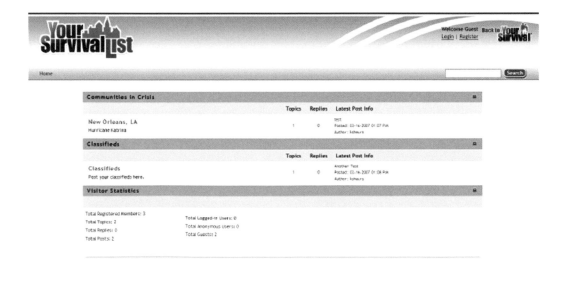

CHERRYPICKING INFO

TO A CERTAIN EXTENT, the level of disaster preparedness you choose is a matter of personal preferences. *Your Survival™* is geared to achieve a solid base level of readiness that will protect you against nearly all the scenarios you're likely to encounter from the most common natural and man-made disasters.

On a scale of 1 to 10, with 1 being completely unprepared and 10 being that bunker with the MREs, *Your Survival™* gives you about a 7. If that describes your family's current level, feel free to skip the "Extra Credit" boxes you'll see sprinkled throughout this guide.

On the other hand, if you desire some more foolproof protection—or just happen to be curious about 55-gallon water drums or have kids who are into MREs and evacuation drills—Extra Credits can make for interesting and helpful reading.

ICONS USED IN THIS GUIDE

We've included the handy symbols below to draw your attention to key bits of information and help you really zero in on what you're looking for.

While *Your Survival™* is filled with thousands of helpful hints, this symbol flags info that even some preparedness veterans may not know.

In addition to all of its other features, yoursurvival.com is your portal to anything else disaster-related on the Web. This icon lets you know about hotlinks on the site that will take you straight to other important sources of information.

This guide has been designed to help get your family prepared as quickly, and cheaply, as possible. But sometimes an item is so essential — or just so innovative — we can't resist recommending you buy it. So we mark it with this doodad.

There's a lot of "bad information" about disaster preparedness. Our Common Myths symbol clues you in to kernels of conventional wisdom that are just plain wrong.

Planning for a "disaster" can seem rather ambiguous compared to planning for 300 mph winds or seismic forces equivalent to an atom bomb.

Chapter 1

IDENTIFYING YOUR RISKS

In This Chapter

✓ Learning about some hazards you probably aren't aware of

✓ Taking a hard look at your property

✓ Assessing your risk for America's most common disasters

IN ONE SENSE, THERE ARE ONLY TWO TYPES OF DISASTERS:

Those that force you to hunker down and those you need to flee. Eighty percent of the advice in Your Survival™ is general and applies to everyone, regardless of where they live or what kind of disaster they're at risk for, whether earthquakes, mudslides, wildfires, tsunamis, or (for some lucky Californians) all of the above. Still, it makes sense to spend some time now thinking about the specific hazards you might face. It will help focus your energies when you come to questions like whether or not you need flood insurance or what kind of improvements you should make to your house. Plus, it's just a great exercise for getting your preparedness crew in the right frame of mind. Planning for a "disaster," after all, can seem rather ambiguous compared to planning for 300 mph winds or seismic forces equivalent to an atom bomb.

NO ONE IS COMPLETELY SAFE

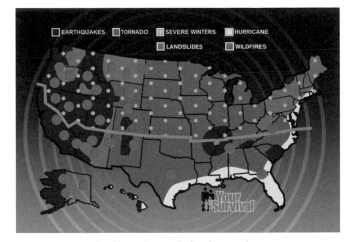

ON THE accompanying *Your Survival*™ DVD, we conduct a preparedness exercise that anyone living in a supposedly "safe" part of the country should find very compelling. As we begin examining the potential hazards, maps of the United States appear and start filling in with colors and patterns coresponding to each of the major threats. A version of what the map looks like when all the hazards are super-imposed on one another appears above. As you can see, not a speck of it is left blank. "It's just a function of living on an increasingly crowded, meteorologically and geologically active planet," says Kathleen Tierney, Ph.D., director of the Natural Hazards Center at the University of Colorado. "Every part of this country has *some* disaster it needs to be concerned about."

Lessons Learned

"We were in the house when the tornado came. We were watching it on TV and it looked like it would miss us. But then it turned. My wife and I grabbed a blanket and our two-and-half-year-old son and got inside our bedroom closet with the blanket over our heads. Next we heard the wind, and then it got louder and LOUDER. We could hear it ripping apart our roof and walls. When it finally stopped, I stood up, and everything was flattened. I said, 'Oh my God, our neighborhood is gone.' And, my wife, who was still crouched down under the blanket with our son, said, 'Oh, honey, I'm sure you're making it worse than it is. I'm sure we can rebuild.' And I said, 'No, you don't understand. Our neighborhood is gone.'"

— *Randy Thurman, 47, Oklahoma City investment advisor, recalling the May 3, 1999, "Billion-Dollar" Tornado*

Some of those are obvious. If you live in California, you don't need *Your Survival™* to tell you that you're at risk for earthquakes. Ditto for South Floridians and hurricanes or Plains Staters and tornadoes. **What's most striking about the map, though, are all the risks that aren't so obvious:**

✔ Although the country's most active earthquake faults lie on the West Coast, major seismic areas do exist in the Southeast. In fact, the most powerful earthquakes ever to strike the continental U.S. occurred along the so-called "New Madrid" fault near Memphis, between 1811 and 1812. Registering more than 8.0 on the Richter scale, some of these tremors were so powerful they caused the Mississippi River to flow *backwards*. Seismologists put the chances of a quake 7.5 or greater hitting the area again sometime in the next 35 years at roughly 25 percent; the chances of one 6.0 or greater at close to 90 percent.

✔ There's a reason Oklahoma, Kansas, and North Texas have earned the nickname "Tornado Alley." However, tornadoes also occur regularly throughout the Midwest, occasionally in the Northeast, and, as we've seen in a peculiarly alarming fashion the past couple seasons, in the Southeast. "The tricky thing about tornadoes in the Southeast," says Kevin Kelleher, deputy director of the National Severe Storms Laboratory in Norman, Oklahoma, "is they tend to hit more at *night*. Especially during the late winter, early spring, they kind of sneak up on you while you're sleeping."

Lessons Learned

"People always ask me, how can you still want to live in New Orleans? I ask them, 'Where am I supposed to go in the United States where there is no weather?' Up north they have blizzards, in the central United States tornadoes, in California it's earthquakes and mudslides. I don't know where they want me to move."

—Joe Gallodoro, 58, insurance agent and grandfather from St. Bernard Parish, Louisiana, who lost his home and workplace to Hurricane Katrina. His elderly father also died in the accompanying flooding at the city's St. Rita's nursing home.

Alex Yuju, 6, standing atop what was left of his family's home in Lakeview, Louisiana, after Hurricane Katrina.

✔ A combination of global warming and the increasing encroachment of development in former wilderness areas has made wildfires one of the nation's fastest growing natural disasters. Large portions of the developed West have become almost like giant tinderboxes. The problem is also acute in portions of the upper Midwest, New England, Georgia, and Florida. In 2006 there were even outbreaks on Staten Island, part of New York City.

✔ In recent years, the Carolinas, Florida, and the Gulf Coast have grabbed most of the hurricane attention. While it's true that severe hurricanes in the Northeast tend to be rarer, they also come with less warning. As Max Mayfield, director of the National Hurricane Center, explains, "The

For an even more thorough look at a specific location's disaster level, check out two resources at yoursurvival.com: Go to the Resources tab and click on USC Database, and you'll be taken to an enormous information depot run by the University of South Carolina that lets you see every significant disaster that's ever occurred in your county, ranked by dollar damage, deaths, and injury. Hit Chemical Scorecard and type in your town in the "facility reports" box to find the lowdown on all the chemical facilities in your area.

hurricanes that make landfall up there are the ones that accelerate very quickly out over the Atlantic." How quickly? The most severe hurricane ever to hit the Northeast, the famous 1938 Category 3 "Long Island Express" that devastated New York City's eastern bedroom communities, sat off the coast of Daytona Beach, Florida, just *24 hours* before hitting.

✔ Landslides and mudslides (essentially a type of landslide with fewer rocks and uprooted trees but more mud) are an often overlooked, especially nasty, hazard. Usually identified with California, they also regularly upend lives along a large swath of the Alleghenies. "The really bad ones," says Paula Gori of the U.S. Geological Survey, "don't just destroy your home; they can carry away your *land*. There's nothing left even to build on. It's a total loss."

✔ Don't forget about snow, ice, thunderstorms, and heat. "People down here in the D.C. area and in the supposedly 'mild' portions of Virginia, Kentucky, Tennessee, and Georgia, are still talking about the 'Storm of the Century' in 1994," recalls veteran FEMA community and family prepared-

ness specialist Ralph Swisher. "Because of all the downed power-lines from the heavy ice, you had 10 million people—including my wife and I—without power for up to 10 days." More recently, severe thunderstorms and heat waves left half a million people in St. Louis and 100,000 in Queens, New York, sweltering without electricity for up to a week during the summer of 2006.

LOCATION LOCATION LOCATION

OF COURSE, disasters aren't just determined by maps of the United States. They're also determined by specific terrain and weather patterns that can change from county to county or even house to house. Now's a good time to take a hard look at your existing home, or to think again about that property you're considering buying.

Seven Questions About Your Property

1. How high does the house sit in relation to the surrounding terrain? Put another way, if your neighborhood was to flood would your house be one of the first or last underwater?

2. Do you know where the dams or dykes are in your area, and what kind of shape they're in?

3. How close is your house to dense brush or other flammable areas?

4. Does it sit on a steep slope that could be prone to landslides?

5. What's the ground underneath the house like? Is it made of bedrock and dense soils that could help absorb the impact of an earthquake, or loose fill that could "liquefy" and open like a giant mouth and swallow up everything you own?

6. How close are you to a nuclear power plant or toxic chemical production or storage facilities?

7. Is the property located near one of the high-profile cities or tourist attractions thought to be likely terrorist targets?

There is a 1 in 10 chance that sometime over the next 30 years the country will experience another massive rupture of the San Andreas fault, similar to the "Big One" that caused the 1906 San Francisco earthquake. This time it's estimated that damages will total $150 billion, and leave 400,000 homeless. There's also a 1 in 4 chance of another big one along a different Bay Area fault line known as the Hayward. Because it runs near the fragile levees and canals that link Northern California's reservoirs to the L.A. basin, this mega-quake could leave 22 million southern Californians without drinking water for weeks or even months.

A WORD ABOUT FLOOD MAPS

HISTORICALLY, FLOODING is the most common and most costly type of disaster in the United States, averaging anywhere from about $2 billion in damages in a typical year to $80 billion in a doozy like 2005. By law, anyone selling a house has to disclose whether it sits in an area at risk for flooding, known as a "flood plain." These areas are awarded a letter: A, B, C, X (used on some maps to lump together B and C), as well as V (for high-velocity waves). A and V are the riskiest. The problem is, these designations are not as precise as they seem, because the information they're based on is often woefully out of date. In coastal areas, erosion of beaches and wetlands may mean that surge zones actually extend hundreds of yards farther inland than what's indicated on the outdated flood maps. In other areas, the maps showing the flooding patterns of rivers and streams may not take into account 20 years or more of new construction and new roads. (Development always brings with it more sewers and storm drains, and more potential for flooding

Photo by Melodi Trevarthen

A satellite image of flooding in New Orleans after Hurricane Katrina.

downstream.) The U.S. Geological Survey has recently undertaken a nation-wide effort to address the issues with these maps. Planning experts suggest you look up the flood map for your neighborhood, usually available online or at the public library. Then look at the date on the map. If it hasn't been updated in the past few years, you may need to "round up" in determining your risk. In other words, if you're looking at a non-updated map and it says you live in a B zone, don't be surprised if you're really in an A. If it says you're just outside the C, you could be a C+ at least.

The five fastest growing counties in Colorado are also the five counties in the state at greatest risk for wildfires.

One of the areas in the United States most vulnerable to storm surge are the densely populated parts of New York City, Brooklyn, Queens, and Long Island, which jut out just beyond the coast of New Jersey. If another storm like the famous 1938 hurricane were to strike, a 30-foot dome of water could crash into an area now home to some 2.5 million people.

SPECIAL REPORT
BIRD FLU AND YOU

IF THE PROJECTIONS are correct, an avian flu pandemic would be unrivaled as a disaster: 150 million dead worldwide; the closure of international borders; mass work absenteeism leading to rampant shortages of food, fuel, and medicine; and a breakdown of the social order on a scale this country has rarely seen. Currently, the avian flu is deadly to birds and humans, but the virus hasn't mutated to the point where it can spread easily via human-to-human contact. It may never make that leap. But even if this bird flu turns out to be a false alarm, we're still at risk for a pandemic flu virus of some kind. Throughout human history, such viruses have killed millions. The most famous flu pandemic was the 1918 Spanish Flu, which killed 50 million worldwide; smaller outbreaks occurred in 1957 and 1968.

"The world is obviosly unprepared or inadequately prepared for the potential of a pandemic."
— *U.S. Health and Human Services Secretary Michael Leavitt, in a recent address to Congress*

There's also the possibility of a terrorist-induced pandemic of smallpox or a similarly destructive biological agent. So don't think of preparing for bird flu as some Chicken Little exercise in hysteria. At the very least, it's an important dress rehearsal for any number of similar threats.

What should you do to prepare? For the most part, you'll already be doing it. All of the preparations contained in *Your Survival*™ will put you in a better position to ride out the shortages and quarantines that would accompany a pandemic. To reach full bird flu readiness, simply step it up a notch: In the next chapter, **where we recommend having a two-week supply of food and water, you could increase that to a three-month supply**, which is how long each of the virus's three "waves" is projected to last. If you have a son or daughter away at college, as you draw up

U.S. hospitals currently only have enough oxygen on hand to meet the expected demand for ventilators in a bird flu pandemic for two or three days.

your evacuation plans, **think about how quickly you could get your child home or into a less crowded environment**. In the medicine kit section, buy several dozen surgical masks, so family members will have enough to wear whenever they venture into a potentially contaminated area. And where we recommend asking your physician for an antibiotic prescription, ask about whether

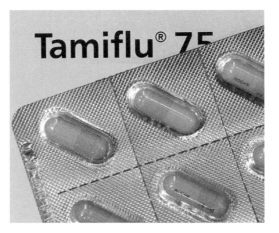

it might make sense for you to **get a prescription for Relenza® or Tamiflu®** antiviral preparations. These powerful antivirals are the world's only two drugs so far proven to combat avian influenza, but they need to be taken within 48 hours of the first onset of symptoms, which is why getting the pills in advance is critical. The U.S. government has specifically discouraged doctors from helping you do this; given the limited supply of the drugs, officials fear there won't be enough for vital public health and emergency personnel. Unfortunately the interests of individual citizens, like you and your family, are a lower priority.

"As a public health official, I know how important it is that we have these drugs for health workers. But to be honest, I also know that if a pandemic occurs and a member of your family gets sick you won't be able to get any," says Mike Osterholm, a University of Minnesota epidemiologist who has emerged as one of the go-to experts on bird flu preparedness issues. "If you can obtain some now, I suggest you should."

THINGS TO REMEMBER

THINGS TO REMEMBER

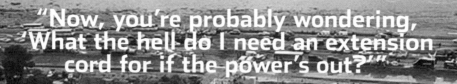

"Now, you're probably wondering, 'What the hell do I need an extension cord for if the power's out?'"

Chapter 2

PLANNING AHEAD

In This Chapter

- ✔ Laying in your supplies
- ✔ Getting your financial affairs and insurance in order
- ✔ Figuring out what home improvements you need
- ✔ Drawing up your communication and evacuation plans

YOU'LL NOTICE THAT THIS IS THE LENGTHIEST CHAPTER BY FAR.

There's a reason for that. Most of what you need to do to prepare for a disaster should be done well in advance of the crisis. Stocking up on supplies, reviewing your insurance policy, making copies of your vital records, and planning your escape routes are all things you want to be doing now when you're calm, the phone circuits are open, and there are no lines at the store—not when the horizon is blackening and the roads are clogged with panicked evacuees. But don't turn this into some month-long, costly project. Aside from whatever disaster-proofing home improvements you

There's also a more tech-savvy way to take stock. Click on <u>Know Your Stuff</u> under the Resources tab at <u>yoursurvival.com</u> to go to the Insurance Information Institute page where you can download the organization's free home-inventorying software. All you need is a digital camera. The software walks you through how to take your photos, and provides a convenient way to organize the images and cost info. Then when you're done, upload the contents onto a flash drive and store it the same way you would the prints. The software works even better now thanks to an upgrade after the institute experienced a huge increase in traffic from across the country in the wake of Hurricane Katrina.

decide to make, you should be able to get through all the preparations outlined in this chapter in a single weekend.

TAKING STOCK

BEFORE YOU can protect yourself from disaster, you need to take stock of everything that's at risk. This is critical if you ever have to put a claim in with your insurance company. It's always harder to collect if you can't at least demonstrate to your insurer exactly what you lost. As Jeanne Salvatore of the Insurance Information Institute puts it, "If your house has been destroyed, and all you remember about your sofa is that it was 'beige,'

you can pretty much count on being reimbursed for your basic, no-frills beige sofa."

The time-honored method of taking stock of your possessions is to go around to every room of your house and take photos. Make a list of all your significant possessions and the estimated cost of each. Receipts are even better if you have them, but not essential. Be sure to include clothes and things inside

Lessons Learned

"The one thing we did right was the Friday night before the storm, I told my wife, who's a photography nut, to stand in the middle of every room and take a picture of every wall. The best one was of my big-screen TV. On the screen you could actually see the satellite image of the storm and the words 'Katrina headed to New Orleans.' Later, the insurance adjustor came out to our house, and she put on her Hazmat suit and goggles and rubber gloves, and she was about to walk inside, when I said, 'Wait a minute, there's something I want you to see.' And I spread all those photos on the hood of my car. She wouldn't have even been able to tell I had a big-screen TV if not for that."

—Joe Gallodoro, St. Bernard Parish, Louisiana

cabinets like dishes and CDs. Get an extra set of prints made, make a copy of your list of possessions and receipts, and store in a pair of folders. Mail one folder to a close friend or relative in a distant city, and store the other with the rest of your vital documents. (See "Getting Your Affairs in Order," page 39.)

STOCKING UP

DISASTERS ALMOST by definition disrupt electricity, knock out water pumping stations, create runs on grocery shelves, and generally uproot us from our usual 21st century lives and plop us down somewhere circa 1890. One key way to absorb their impact is to be able to go with the flow for the duration of the time warp, and for that you need the right kind of supplies. You can easily accumulate some of the items you need

while doing your regular shopping; others, like hurricane lanterns and head-lamps, require more foresight. But, fortunately, disaster shopping isn't too different from shopping for a camping trip. Just hit your favorite outdoors store, pick a safe and convenient pantry, closet, or corner of the basement, and stock up.

Sample Disaster Grocery List for the Typical Family of Four

✔ 16 cans tuna, salmon, and/or sardines
✔ 12 cans chicken
✔ 4 cans chili
✔ 4 cans baked beans
✔ 4 cans other beans
✔ 12 cans soups and stews
✔ 16 cans fruit
✔ 6 boxes pasta
✔ 1 large bag rice
✔ 1 jar pickles
✔ 1 16-oz bottle cooking oil
✔ 3 cartons granola, breakfast or power bars
✔ 2 bags dried fruit
✔ 2 40-oz jars peanut butter
✔ 2 jars jelly
✔ 4 boxes crackers
✔ 3 gallons powdered milk

✔ 1 can coffee
✔ 2 boxes oatmeal
✔ 6 boxes dried cereal
✔ 2 boxes pancake mix
✔ 8 rolls paper towels
✔ 7 boxes garbage bags
✔ 2 cans dried nuts
✔ 1 package each paper plates, bowls, cups, utensils
✔ 12 rolls toilet paper
✔ 2 bottles hand sanitizer
✔ Tube toothpaste, toothbrushes, soap, large bottle, shampoo
✔ 1 large bag dried pet food and cat litter (for families with pets)
✔ Matches
✔ Whistle
✔ Playing cards, board games

FOOD AND SUNDRIES

THE TRADITIONAL PREPAREDNESS ADVICE was to have enough food and water to last three days. Since the devastating hurricanes and other extended power outages of the past few years, that advice has been revised upward to at least two weeks—or up to three months, if you're concerned about bird flu. (See "Special Report: Bird Flu and You," page 20.) To prevent spoilage, rotate the supplies in with the food you're eating every six months, then restock. On the previous page is a sample grocery list for a typical family of four. The same checklist minus the quantities can be found in the accompanying Express Planner card for you to adapt to the precise head count of your family and take with you to the store.

WATER

LAY IN A TWO-WEEK supply of this necessity; figure on at least a gallon per person, per day. Unlike a food stockpile, this amount of water can take up *a lot* of room. The choice is yours: Find the space, or be prepared for some anxious moments later if you have to run out to the 7-Eleven® store before the shelves are empty, or if you have to resort to more makeshift methods, like tapping your water heater or collecting rainwater (described in Chapter 5, "Immediate Aftermath," page 87).

A great backup to a bottled water supply is a water filter. It will remove toxins and bacteria in the event your tap water is contaminated or you have to rely on external sources like rain or stream water. We recommend a model like the Katadyn Hiker™, for $55.

Caffeine withdrawal can be unpleasant, with symptoms mimicking the flu. Keep a jar of instant coffee with your disaster supplies, or invest in a metal coffee pot that can withstand the extreme temperatures of a grill.

GAS GRILL

IF YOU DON'T have a portable propane grill, it could be time to get one. The outdoor portable propane-powered grill is to the average disaster-stranded suburban family what the campfire was to the cowboy: the center of social activity, a ready source of heat, and the means to cook food. But, remember: Always keep at least one full tank of propane in reserve as a disaster spare.

PORTABLE HEATER

MOST HOME furnaces today have electric starters and fans, so a cold-weather storm that's bad enough to knock out power lines can also knock out heat. Owning at least one portable propane heater such as a Mr. Heater® "Portable Buddy" ($87.50) is basic disaster management—and that goes for all parts of the country, including supposedly "mild" portions of the South.

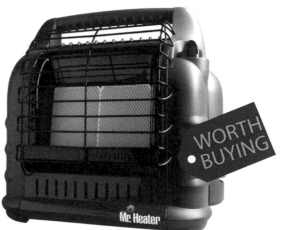

Lessons Learned

"The one thing no one ever thinks about in a disaster is an extension cord. Now, you're probably wondering, 'What the hell do I need an extension cord for if the power's out?' Because when it finally does start coming back on, it's not like it comes back on every-where, all at once. After Hurricane Wilma we got our electricity turned back on two weeks before our neighbor. Luckily, we had some long extension cords, so his wife, who's dia-betic, could start refrigerating her insulin again."

—Pat Jordan, 65, Fort Lauderdale-based author who, along with his wife and neighbors, survived for four days without running water and 10 days without power after Hurricane Wilma, in October 2005

OTHER APPLIANCES

LOOK AT ALL of the other essential appliances in your house that run on electricity. If the power goes, have manual or battery-operated versions as backups. At a minimum, you should have a manual can opener and a crank or transistor radio, and probably a portable Game Boy® video game for the kids. Florida hurricane veterans also swear by their battery-operated TVs. "My wife got a little black-and-white screen for $15," says National Hurricane Center Director Max Mayfield. "She says it helps if she can at least see where the storm is."

LIGHT

IT'S AMAZING how many tech-savvy people who always have the latest iPod® device or high-definition TV rely on a flimsy, decades-old, plastic flashlight. Spend the money and invest in a powerful flashlight that can withstand hours of use and abuse during an emergency. For $35, Mag Instrument has a new LED bulb version with triple the battery life of its regular 3 D-cell-battery model. (One of the biggest problems with standard flashlights is how quickly they deplete batteries.) You'll also want to pick up a couple of battery-powered headlamps, so you don't have to juggle a flashlight while you're trying to grill dinner. Big Bang and Princeton Tectonics make reliable, low-end LED models starting at around $19. Also, stock up on some battery-operated LED hurricane lamps for ambient lighting to read and cook by. Garrity makes a serviceable 3 C-cell lamp with a 200-hour battery lifespan, for $40.

BATTERIES

EVEN LED LIGHTS need to have their batteries replaced occasionally. Count on at least three refills of batteries per battery-operated gadget. Be sure to double-check which kind (D, C, AA, etc.) goes in each. And remember to replace all the batteries in your disaster supplies once a year before they lose their juice. (For a complete Planning Ahead maintenance schedule, see page 57.)

RADIO

IN THE SOUTHWEST'S "Tornado Alley," many families have what's known as a NOAA® battery-operated weather radio. It's kept on 24 hours a day, seven days a week, and normally remains silent. But the instant the National Weather Service issues a warning for their area the radio emits a piercing beeping sound. With a premium membership at yoursurvival.com, you'll soon be able to get a similar life-saving service—which also alerts you to hurricanes and other severe storms—sent directly to your computer, cell phone, and wireless PDA. Another option is to pick

up a NOAA™ radio on the Amazon.com® or Buy.com™ websites. (For about $50, it will come with built-in AM/FM frequencies.) Look for a brand with "S.A.M.E." technology, which enables you to focus the alert on your immediate vicinity. Otherwise, acknowledges Kevin Kelleher of the National Severe Storms Laboratory, its tendency to go off for storms several counties away "can get pretty tiresome pretty fast."

In earthquake country, where the power can go out very suddenly, a lot of people prefer the kind of rechargeable wall-socket-mounted flashlight that turns on automatically as soon as the grid goes down. Even if you don't live in California, consider picking up a few of the discreetly sized Garrity® Rechargeable Flashlights ($24) to stand sentry in everyone's bedrooms

PLASTIC AND DUCT TAPE

AFTER THE anthrax scare in 2001, Americans rushed out and bought plastic sheeting and duct tape to safeguard themselves at home. Since then we've realized that the technological hurdles to a wide-scale biological attack are higher than originally feared. But that doesn't mean some people shouldn't still be prepared. If you live in New York City or Washington, DC, near the Sears Tower or another high-profile potential terrorist target, or within about 10 miles of a toxic chemical facility or 50 miles of a nuclear power plant, you should pick out an aboveground room in your house that could serve as your family's temporary containment shelter. According to FEMA, the room should be big enough for about 10 square feet of floor space per person, which will provide sufficient air for up to five hours. Then buy enough sheeting and duct tape, to be able to seal each window, door, and vent. And don't forget a pair of scissors!

HOSE AND LADDER

LIKE PLASTIC sheeting and duct tape, this is another semi-specialized set of tools that you may not need but could be glad you have. As wildfires approach an area, there's usually enough time for some last-minute precautions to defend your property. A long, sturdy extension ladder and equivalent-length hose will allow you to climb up to your roof and wet it down, which can make a big difference when the flames start licking at your neighbor's house.

GAS SHUT-OFF WRENCH

SHUT-OFF WRENCHES are those hard-rubber nonadjustable tools with the narrow rectangular opening in the center, that you may have seen at the hardware store. Useful anywhere, they are especially crucial in Tornado
Alley and earthquake-prone areas, where twisters and quakes tend to rupture gas lines, which in turn tend to explode. You can usually find one for about $20.

The Gasoline-Powered Generator Question

IT'S ONE OF the first items many people think of when they think of disaster preparedness—and a pricey one at that. So you may be surprised to learn that some hard-core disaster types aren't especially fond of generators.

"I'm not a big fan," says "Captain" Dave Reeder, creator of Captain Dave's Survival Center, a popular survivalist gear website. "For one, they're not cheap. Two, I'm always afraid that if I keep that much gasoline around, my house might blow up.

Three, I know too many people who buy one, don't use it for the longest time, and then there's finally a real crisis—and it doesn't start."

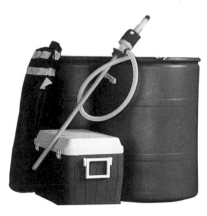

Whether you should get one depends on your level of disaster risk, how much you want to invest in your preparedness plan, and how critical it is to you to not experience an interruption in power. For instance, if a member of your household is diabetic and needs to refrigerate insulin, that places you in a more urgent category than the family with a 15-year-old who can't live without her hair dryer. Coleman® produces a relatively inexpensive ($480) portable model, the Powermate Pulse™, which generates up to three-and-a-half hours of electricity per gallon of gasoline. For $2,500 to $4,000 you can also get what's known as a "standby" system, which is hardwired into your home's electrical system and runs off your town's natural gas or propane lines. Coleman®, Generac®, and Onan® are some of the better brands.

Water, Water Everywhere

GIVEN THE VITAL importance of water and the difficulties in storing it, a compelling case can be made for something a bit extreme: 55-gallon water drums. If you have a garage, storage shed, or reinforced basement (filled, the drums weigh 400 pounds each), you can create your own personal reservoir.

At Captain Dave's website (click on 55-Gal Water Drums under the Resources tab at yoursurvival.com), you can pick up two plastic drums for less than $100 (plus $80 shipping). And remember to order the $15 hand pump. Because even with proper chlorination (one teaspoon of bleach per 10 gallons), you need to empty out and replace the water every year.

STOCKING YOUR EMERGENCY MEDICINE KIT

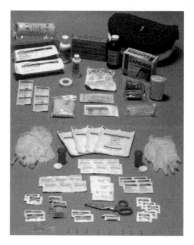

AS DISASTER-PREPAREDNESS has gone more mainstream, several disaster-specific first-aid kits have appeared on pharmacy shelves (the Department of Homeland Security even sponsors one). "But none of them are really optimal," explains Dr. Susan Briggs, a trauma surgeon at Massachusetts General Hospital. As head of the International Medical Surgical Response Team for the East Coast, Briggs headed the federal government's medical response to the Ground Zero terrorist attacks and Hurricane Katrina, and has worked virtually every kind of natural disaster. Her problem with the mass-marketed kits, she explains, is they fail to include the most essential elements of any home emergency medicine stockpile: Your family's medical records and prescriptions. "The biggest health threat after Katrina wasn't the spread of disease from dead bodies. It was the inability of people to get their medications. You had so many people who couldn't get to their insulin or blood-pressure medications, or else didn't know the dose they were on."

That's why Briggs suggests you forego the $30 you would have spent on a pre-packaged kit and spend it instead on your own, tailored to your family's medical needs. Use the following checklist as your guide. To waterproof your kit put batches of like items inside plastic Ziploc® bags. As with your food-stockpile list, a copy of the list can also be found in your Express Planner card.

Once you get your containment shelter gear together, try to store it in a closet in the room where you plan to use it. When the toxic cloud is approaching your house, lugging your rolls of plastic up from the basement is one trip you don't want to make.

Dr. Susan Briggs'
Ultimate Disaster Emergency Medicine Kit

✔ A laminated list of every family member's allergies, chronic medical conditions, and prescriptions, including dosages, plus a week's worth of spare doses for each medication

✔ An official "yellow card" vaccination record for each family member, available from most doctors' offices or any travel medicine clinic. Simply call your physician for help in filling them out. Each card should include the current status of everyone's shots. Anyone not up to date on tetanus should get a booster, and anyone with special skills who might be called on as a first responder should consider getting vaccinated for hepatitis A and B.

✔ A prescription for Ciprofloxacin®, usually available from your doctor. The most common risk for infection in a disaster is common traveler's-type diarrhea from waterborne bacteria, and Cipro is the best antibiotic for knocking it out.

✔ Two 8 oz. bottles of electrolyte drinks, like Gatorade® brand

✔ Small packages or bottles of anti-diarrheals (Lomotil® or Imodium®), antacids, antihistamine, acetaminophen, and ibuprofen

✔ EpiPen®, injector to prevent anaphylactic shock in the event of a severe allergic reaction

✔ An assortment of bandages, including two dozen Band-Aids® brand bandages, a half dozen sterile gauze pads, one conforming gauze roll, one Ace® brand wrap, and one roll of 2-inch adhesive tape

✔ Betadyne® anticeptic, a box of antiseptic wipes and germicidal hand wipes, a tube of anti-bacterial ointment (Neosporin® or Bacitracin® brand), and two pairs of non-sterile latex gloves

✔ Cold pack

✔ Small scissors, tweezers, and a thermometer

✔ Generic soft water-resistant backpack, for easy transport in a "bug-out" situation (see page 53)

Lessons Learned

"Before the storm, we went into the office and covered the computers in plastic. We figured if the roof leaked they'd be okay. And the woman who did the back-up put the storage drive on a top shelf. Well, let me tell you, in 15 feet of water there is no top shelf. Afterward, I sent the hard drives out to this company that retrieves data off of damaged drives and they said, 'Mister, there is no amount of money that can retrieve the data off your computer after what they've gone through.'"

— Joe Gallodoro, St. Bernard Parish, Louisiana

"The biggest health threat after Katrina wasn't the spread of disease from dead bodies. It was the inability of people to get their medications. You had so many people who couldn't get to their insulin or blood-pressure medications, or else didn't know the dose they were on."

BACKING UP

IF YOU'RE STILL relying on a single computer hard drive to store your photos, music, work files, school projects, and financial records, then even in the absence of an earthquake, hurricane, or dirty bomb, you're a digital disaster waiting to happen. Use this opportunity to get in the habit of backing up all your essential computer files every week. Copy them onto a flash drive and store them with the rest of your physical files (see "Getting Your Affairs in Order," on the next page). And keep an eye out  for announcements at <u>yoursurvival.com</u> about the launch of our data protection service, which will give premium members the option of having their files automatically uploaded to a secure remote backup facility.

COMMON MYTHS

"You should keep your important papers in a fire-resistant metal box."

It's true, a metal box will usually survive a fire, but that doesn't mean what's in it will. The temperature of wildfires is so high that victims who place their papers in these containers often come across their boxes afterwards, open them up—and find ashes inside. You're better off going with a plastic box. At least it'll be semi-resistant to rain and water, and it's lighter in an escape. Target sells a Rubbermaid® 9x9x12-inch tote with a handle on top for about $10.

GETTING YOUR AFFAIRS IN ORDER

J **UST ONE OF** the many hard, hard lessons of Hurricane Katrina was the fragility of vital records. People lost the deeds to their houses, titles to their cars, retirement account statements, wills, marriage certificates, divorce settlements. And if that wasn't bad enough, in many cases the deed offices, motor vehicle bureaus, county clerks offices, and brokerage and law firms that could have provided the information were themselves six feet underwater. It took some folks weeks just to verify for their insurance companies and the relief agencies where they'd lived. The lesson here is simple: You should always have all your vital financial records well-organized and at your fingertips. Make a copy of everything. You can do this using either non-tech methods (a pen, the blank financial record forms in your Express Planner card, a photocopy machine) or digital ones (a scanner or digital camera and the online forms at **yoursurvival.com**). If you go the former route, send copies to a close friend or relative in a distant city; if you go digital, they can be stored at **yoursurvival.com**'s secure server, where you can access them from anywhere. Then keep the hard-copy originals in some sort of sturdy, lightweight, waterproof container with a handle, and store it with the rest of your disaster supplies. These documents should include:

✔ Your Survival™ Financial Records Form listing the company and account numbers for all checking, savings, stock, college, and retirement accounts, as well as the company, policy numbers and name of insured for all home, life, car, disability, and health insurance policies

✔ All birth, death, and marriage certificates

✔ Divorce and child custody papers

✔ Passports, military records, social security cards

✓ Mortgage/property deeds

✓ Car titles

✓ Wills, powers of attorney, and living wills

✓ Last three years of federal tax returns. Since these can be cumbersome to copy or scan, you can skip including in your remote set. But definitely keep one set here. As explained in the last chapter, certain little-known provisions in the tax code can help make up for insurance shortfalls, but you need your tax records to take advantage of them. Having a set on hand will save you time waiting for the IRS to mail yours to you.

✓ Important home-improvement records

✓ Flash drives of important computer files (at least until the Your Survival™ premium-member automatic backup service goes live)

✓ Folder or flashdrive of photos inventorying your valuables for insurance purposes

✓ $500 or more in cash

SIZING UP YOUR INSURANCE

THIS MAY BE the area of greatest importance that people know the least about. Some people get themselves in trouble because they assume that just having insurance entitles them to coverage if something goes wrong. Others hear the horror stories associated with Hurricane Katrina and other recent disasters and think it doesn't matter whether they have insurance or not. In reality, neither view is particularly helpful when planning for a disaster. An insurance policy isn't a form of entitlement or some capricious instrument of torture; it's a contract with specific language detailing what one party will— or will not—pay under a whole range of circumstances.

If you haven't already, you need to pull out the contract you agreed to when you began paying your homeowner's premiums, and read it, preferably in collaboration with your insurance agent. Anything you don't understand you need to ask about. If you don't like the answers you're hearing, you need to consider updating the policy, or maybe even switching to a different carrier. You'll want to focus on the questions on the following page.

Eight Questions for Your Insurance Agent

1. "Will my policy pay for the guaranteed replacement cost or just the replacement cost of damages to my house?"

The standard "replacement cost" homeowner's policy isn't what it sounds like. Such a policy will only pay to repair or replace your house up to a certain dollar amount specified in the policy, usually based on rebuilding costs at the time the policy was written. To make sure you will have enough money to replace your house at current building prices, you can check on your limit each year and pay more to raise it, or buy an "inflation guard" that raises it automatically. But even then you might get caught short, because building costs often soar after a major disaster. (In New Orleans, for example, homebuilding costs have gone from an average of $100 per square foot before Katrina to $135.) To keep pace with that kind of hike you need to buy either "extended replacement cost" coverage (which can pay anywhere from 20 to 80 percent above the specified limit) or, better yet, "guaranteed replacement cost," which guarantees to put your house back together the way it was regardless of how much rebuilding costs.

2. "What kind of contents coverage do I have?"

The contents of a house are always insured separately from the structure itself, and always only up to some specified limit. Here again, it's important to check and update your limit. Plus, you should check the formula your policy will use to reimburse you for your possessions: "replacement cost contents" coverage pays to replace items with the same items; "cash value" coverage will only reimburse you for the value of the items less depreciation.

"Talk about your woulda, coulda, shoulda. For another several hundred dollars a year, I could have collected another $250,000."

3. "Do I need flood insurance?"

Most homeowner's policies typically cover damage from wind, fire, rain, snow, ice, and tornadoes—but not flood. For that you need to buy supplemental flood insurance. If you live in an officially designated flood plain, you'll be required to buy it by your mortgage company. Just because you aren't required to get it, though, doesn't necessarily mean you shouldn't. If you live in any sort of coastal or other area at risk for flooding, review the previous chapter about assessing your flood risks, and keep in mind that flood plains are often arbitrary. Granted, Katrina is an extreme example, but even with the extraordinary measures being taken by the Louisiana Recovery and Mississippi Development authorities, there are thousands of Gulf Coast residents like Kathy Hebert who are now out hundreds of thousands of dollars because they weren't "required" to buy flood insurance. Available through your usual insurance agent from the federal flood insurance program, flood insurance can run anywhere from $300 to $1,000 per year for up to $250,000 worth of coverage.

4. "Do I need more flood insurance?"

You're not required to buy flood insurance on your contents, but anyone at risk for flood would be crazy not to. A max of $100,000 worth of coverage is available from the same federal program for roughly $200 to $800 a year. In addition, if you live in a higher-priced home, you should consider purchasing "excess" flood coverage on both your house and contents over and above what the government offers. A growing number of higher-end private insurers, including AIG, Liberty Mutual, and Chubb, offer such coverage.

Lessons Learned

"I thought about getting flood insurance. Every time we had a bad storm, I'd think to myself, 'Should we get it?' But we were renters, so it wasn't required. Plus, our place was about 100 yards from the beach, and it was up this little hill. So I always figured we'd be okay."

— *Christi Covington, 35, who had no flood insurance when Hurricane Katrina's 30-foot tidal surge swept away her entire Long Beach, Mississippi, apartment building, including all her possessions.*

5. "What about earthquake or mudslide insurance?"

If you live in an area at risk for these hazards, you need to understand that your insurance options are limited. Regular homeowner's polices don't cover earthquake damage. You can buy separate earthquake coverage, and if you live in certain areas, it's a costly but necessary expense you probably need to make. But in some of the high-risk areas of California, the deductibles have gotten so high and insurers have started imposing so many restrictions that even some people whose homes were destroyed by past earthquakes have begun going without.

The situation regarding landslides and mudslides is even trickier. Although

landslide insurance is technically available from certain select insurers, it's so expensive and difficult to collect on, it's rarely recommended. Your best bet is to buy flood insurance, and then just hope that if a mudslide occurs it contains a high enough percentage of water for the Federal Emergency Management Agency (which coincidentally also administers the flood insurance program) to rule that it constitutes a "flood."

Lessons Learned

"I sell flood insurance. So I knew I could have gotten excess flood coverage on my home and I still didn't get it. Talk about your woulda, coulda, shoulda. Because for another several hundred dollars a year, I could have collected another $250,000."

—Joe Gallodoro, St. Bernard Parish, New Orleans

6. "Are there any other specific provisions I should consider?"

Yes. For instance, most people have no idea they can buy "sump pump insurance" (in the event of heavy rains that your sump pump can't handle) and "sewer backup insurance" (to cover damage from sewer backups). People who live in older houses may want to purchase "building ordinance insurance," which pays the extra costs associated with bringing a damaged older home up to current building codes.

7. "How much is all this going to cost?"

Insurance companies are in the business of managing their risk, too. Generally, any additional protections will cost you more money. In some cases, like basic flood insurance, the difference may be just a few hundred dollars a year; in others, like trying to buy guaranteed replacement coverage in a particularly high-risk area, it may run into the thousands. In some parts of the country, like along the beaches of South Florida, private insurers won't even write the coverage, and you may be forced into certain government-backed "risk pools," which may help keep premiums down, but come with unavoidable restrictions.

8. "So bottom line: Do I have enough?"

As you're finishing your risk-benefit analysis, keep in mind one last little cruel irony about disaster insurance: if you don't have enough, it sometimes is like not having any at all. That's because you won't be the only one who has dibs on your insurance settlement. When an insurance company settles a major claim, it typically makes out the check jointly to the policyholder and the mortgage company that has the lien on the house. If your house is destroyed, your mortgage company no longer has the same collateral backing up its loan, and has the right to demand that you use your insurance settlement to pay off your mortgage. In New Orleans, lots of people who tried to save a couple of hundred dollars a year by buying just $100,000 or $150,000 of flood coverage on a $300,000 or $400,000 home now have a paid-off mortgage on an empty lot worth a fraction of what they paid for it. And not a cent of insurance money to put toward rebuilding.

DISASTER-PROOFING YOUR HOME

IN DISASTER CIRCLES, making physical improvements to your home is known as "mitigation." It can include everything from using Quake Hold™ putty, which keeps breakables from toppling off shelves, to installing special straps that prevent your roof from blowing off in a hurricane or tornado. Fortunately, most of these measures, short of building a full-scale tornado safe room, are inexpensive. At the 2006 International Builders' Show in Orlando, an enormous array of new disaster products were on display, from special nails that can't be pulled out of wood, no matter how strong the wind, to solar-energy-producing roof shingles that would definitely come

in handy during a blackout. Because such measures are highly dependent on location, at this point we suggest you pop in the Your Survival™ DVD and click on the appropriate disaster under "Disaster-Proofing Your Home" for a detailed description of the mitigation strategies most pertinent to your situation. But there are a handful of strategies everyone should consider:

✔ If you don't have a sump pump, talk to a contractor about whether you should get one. (If the answer is yes, buy one with a battery backup so it will

COMMON MYTHS

"You need to waterproof your basement walls."

Save your money, says Dave McLellan, respected building consultant and author of *The National Home Maintenance Manual*. "Home owners have literally spent thousands of dollars and hours trying to coat the inside walls of basements. But the coating flakes off because of the water pressure behind it."

keep pumping through a power outage.) And if you already have one, regularly check to make sure it works. To test it, fill the sump using a bucket until the pump switches on—or doesn't.

✔ Talk to a landscaper about steps you can take to improve the drainage on your property and protect against standing water and mudslides. In a more altruistic vein, ask him about things you can do to limit the runoff from your house onto other people's property, such as installing porous driveway paving stones or an underground catchment pond.

✔ Some "hurricane" mitigation techniques are so cheap and easy that almost anyone exposed to heavy wind should think about employing them. Shingles with a high wind rating, a must in hurricane and tornado country, are also just a nice insurance policy against standard-variety gusts. Hurricane clips are simple 3-inch metal plates that you nail into the corners of your joists to increase the stability of your roof. Wind-resistant garage doors can help safeguard your lawn equipment and cars. Well anchored soffits keep wind and water from getting underneath your eaves and into your attic. Well-pruned trees are less likely to get blown down onto your house.

If you live in an area at risk for wildfires (and, increasingly, that seems to include almost every region of the country), start by regularly cleaning your gutters and clearing dead brush from under your deck and around your home. Next, check to be sure you have a 50-foot "defensible space" of grass or loosely spaced trees and shrubs free of underbrush with occasional firebreaks, such as driveways and walkways. Within five feet of the house, use only nonflammable landscaping materials such as rocks, pavers, annuals, and perennials with a high moisture content. Some trees and shrubs are also more fire-resistant than others. Talk to a landscaper about how yours stack up or simply click on Firewise Plant List under the Resources tab at yoursurvival.com.

✓ To prevent post-disaster water stains on ceilings, each spring inspect your roof for curled or loose shingles and sealant. Re-glue or replace damaged shingles and reapply sealant to any cracks or holes.

✓ Whenever buying a house, hire a building inspector or structural engineer to inspect it for safety, structural integrity, and—this is critical— differences or variations from current build-ing codes. For instance, Florida and California have some of the country's most stringent building codes when it comes to hurricanes and earth-quakes, but that's usually only for houses built after the codes were passed. Older houses, no matter how vulnerable, are almost always grandfathered in until someone starts undertaking renovations that require permits—at which point it can get mighty costly.

In California, where independent schools remain exempt from the state's strict earthquake codes, there are still more than 50 private schools made of un-reinforced masonry, or URMs, also known in local building circles as "FRPs," for "future rubble piles."

The next time you need to replace your roof or siding, ask your contractor about the new "cement-board" siding or shingles. Not only are they impervious to fire, to the naked eye they look exactly like painted wood siding or shakes.

"Media companies are pushing you to have a single communication source. They want you to make all your calls on your cell phone, or to use your high-speed cable for your TV, computer, and phones. That's exactly what increases your exposure in a disaster."

DEVISING YOUR COMMUNICATIONS PLAN

DISASTERS PLAY havoc with communications systems. Cell phone towers get toppled by high winds, switching stations and underground cables get engulfed by fire and flood, circuits get jammed by the surges of callers desperately trying to get in touch with loved ones. Gil Miller, of Mitretek, a renowned science and engineering think tank, has spent 30 years advising government agencies and private employers on how to make their phones and Internet services disaster-ready. What he tells them boils down to pretty much the same advice he would give you and your family: Have a variety of communication devices. "Media companies are pushing you to have a single communication source. They want you to make all your calls on your cell phone, or to use your high speed cable for your TV, computer, and phones. That's exactly what increases your exposure in a disaster," explains Miller. "The more forms of communication you use, the less likely all of them will go down." With that in mind, see Miller's tips on the next page for building a diverse disaster-proof communication system.

Get everyone in your family to punch the acronym ICE (for "In Case of Emergency") into their cell phone along with the number of the person you'd want contacted if they're injured and can't respond. Started by a British paramedic in 2005 (and really jump-started by the July 2005 London terrorist bombing), ICE is increasingly recognized by police, fire, and ambulance crews on this side of the pond.

Remember when you were a kid planning for an imaginary disaster and a walkie-talkie was always involved? Well, it still is. Today's basic units, like Radio Shack's™ GMRS/FRS ($25), work within six miles on standard batteries. They can be an effective means of communication during short forays for additional supplies or if family members evacuate in separate cars.

THE YOUR SURVIVAL™ SECURE FAMILY COMMUNICATIONS PLAN

1. You'll need to get news, information, and advisories from authorities. For this, there is no better alternative than a simple transistor radio or a NOAA® weather radio with built-in AM receiver.

2. To alert others to your location and condition, use a cell phone with text messaging capabilities. Because of the narrower bandwidth required for text messaging, it's more likely that texts will get through (use a simple "I am OK" or "Need help"), even when calls can't be completed. You should also keep a corded telephone in your house, since it runs on the phone company's power source. While these circuits can still jam, they have a better chance of operating during a power outage— which immediately knocks out cordless phones.

3. Another way of bypassing local lines, towers and poles is with the latest Internet access from your satellite TV provider. A dish email service using one of the new supersize "2x3" dishes and a well-charged laptop would theoretically allow you to communicate through any disaster. But in a hurricane you'll need to remember to temporarily take down your big dish before the wind kicks up.

4. Oftentimes in a disaster it's easier to call long distance than it is to call locally. So think about a friend or relative who lives out of town who can be your family's point person in case you're not together when disaster strikes. Then make sure every family member carries the person's contact info with them at all times.

5. Decide ahead of time on a place to meet and a plan of action for circling the herd. Many New Yorkers will always remember that panicked feeling on September 11, when one spouse was stranded at work, another was at home, the kids were at school, and no family member had any way to get in touch with any other. After that experience, a group of four New York families created a "family circle." Each parent has the home, work, and cell phone number of every other parent along with three contacts outside of their area. Should an evacuation take place during school hours, the

WORTH BUYING

parents carry permission slips in their cars that give them the authority to remove another family's children from the schools they attend. As an added level of security, every circle member also has a password known only to them and the school administrators that lets them remove the kids if the permission slips have been lost.

EXTRA CREDIT

Be the First Responder on Your Block

When Gil Miller, a telecom specialist with Washington, DC–based Mitretek, advises first responders, whose calls absolutely must get through, he always recommends a satellite phone. Sat phones are the big guns of disaster communications: Powered by batteries with heavy charge capacity, they beam directly up to satellites, completely bypassing all the jammed and damaged equipment down here on earth. But they're not cheap. Even a low-end reconditioned Globalstar® or Iridium® brand phones costs about $400, which can add up quickly if you plan on uplinking the whole family. And even with Globalstar's discount "emergency" calling plan (just $30 a month), each call runs $1.50 a minute. "I guess if price is no object you could get a sat phone for everybody to carry around with them, and then just make sure they don't use it except in an emergency," says Miller. "You'd certainly be covered that way."

Lessons Learned

"It was after the 1999 Billion-Dollar Tornado went through here that I decided to build a safe room in my house. I kind of went all out: 8-inch concrete walls with rebar, the whole bit. I probably spent close to $7,000. Part of my thinking was my mother-in-law lives down the street. I had visions of her stopping by in the next tornado and saying, 'Okay, I'm taking the kids off to the shelter.' Of course, now the problem is, she has a key to my safe room. Not long ago, my wife and I were out to dinner and tornadoes were passing through the area and my cell phone rings. It's my mother-in-law. 'Hope you don't mind,' she says, 'the neighbors and I are all down in the safe room.'"

— Kevin Kelleher, deputy director, National Severe Storms Laboratory, Norman, Oklahoma

PETS

SOME OF THE most heartbreaking images from recent disasters were of all the pets left behind. Pet owners need to do a little advance planning now to make sure they don't face some excruciating decisions later. Talk to your neighbors about setting up a four-legged version of the same sort of Family Circle plan described on page 50. Also, as you start making your "evacuation" plans (see "Plotting Your Escape Route," page 55) keep in mind that most shelters don't allow animals, but some areas have begun to set up special "pet shelters." Ask your veterinarian if he knows of one near you. Hotels are another good option. You'd be surprised at how many suspend their usual rules during a disaster and allow feline and canine check-ins.

If you haven't yet registered your dog or cat with a micro-chipping service, now is a good time to do so. For as little as $100, your vet will place a small microchip under the scruff of its neck that lets anyone with a scanner determine who the owner is. That way, if you do end up getting separated, at least there's a better chance for a joyous reunion.

"I could have strangled him! He must have had 50 DVDs and video games in there—but no clothes!"

ASSEMBLING YOUR "BUG-OUT" BAGS

THERE MAY COME a time in a disaster when no matter how much care you've dedicated to fortifying your home and stockpiling supplies you may need to leave it all behind and just get the heck out—"bug out" in disaster parlance. In that case, you'll want to grab whatever few essentials you'll need on the road, and fast. Which is where the bug-out bag comes into play. To create bug-out bags simply stuff a backpack for each family member with the items on the following page, and store them with the rest of your supplies. Also get in the habit of storing your family's sleeping bags nearby, along with a handful of other items that could be useful on the road, such as a couple of small tube tents, a leash, and small bag of pet food. That way, the entire family can sling their bug-out bags over their shoulders, grab the med kit, vital financial records box, tents, and sleeping bags, and just go.

Lessons Learned

"When we evacuated, we told all the children to pack and get ready to go, but we were in such a hurry I didn't really have a chance to check what they brought. Then we get to Houston and my 16-year-old unpacks his suitcase and it's full of DVDs and video games. I could have strangled him! He must have had 50 DVDs and video games in there—but no clothes!"

— *Deborah Irabor, 42, mother of three and co-owner with her husband, Mark, of a chain of New Orleans daycare centers, who evacuated with her family from Hurricane Katrina*

Sample Bug-Out Bag

✓ A change of durable clothes suitable for layering (T-shirt, flannel shirt, etc.), including season-appropriate jacket and other outerwear

✓ A pair of comfortable already broken-in shoes

✓ A couple of extra pairs of socks and underwear

✓ Quart of water

✓ Handful of healthy snacks and energy bars

✓ Spare glasses or contact lenses and solution

✓ Personal toiletries

✓ Stuffed animal

✓ Deck of cards

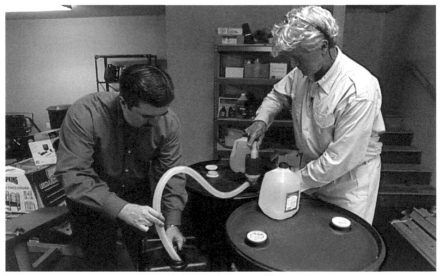

"Captain" Dave helps Dr. Bob tap a 55-gallon water drum.

Lessons Learned

"I'm not a big believer in making your family do drills. I think one of the best ways to practice is to just go camping. It gets everyone used to operating without power, cooking over an open fire, refining the contents of their bug-out bags—pretty much all the skills you need after a disaster. Plus, it's also just a lot more socially acceptable at work on Monday morning to tell your co-workers you went camping, rather than admitting you spent all weekend practicing your disaster drill."

— "Captain" Dave Reeder, 42, father of three and online survivalist gear retailer and guru

THE BUGGED-OUT SUV

THINK OF YOUR car bug-out kit as a very mini, car-based version of your usual basement stockpile, for those times when your family is stranded on the road. It should include a flashlight, a day or so of nonperishable meals and snacks, a gallon of water, blankets, some additional jackets and spare items of clothing, plus a jack, jumper cables, tire-patch kit, and signal flares. If you own a pick-up, a metal lockbox would be the perfect place to store it; if not, any sort of metal or plastic container will do.

PLOTTING YOUR ESCAPE ROUTE

IN ANY BUG-OUT situation, you're always better off if you've rehearsed in your mind where you plan to bug out to. It's less a matter of memorizing the official evacuation routes (because inevitably such info will be all over the airways and the police will be out in force directing you onto the appropriate highways) than deciding where you and your family would head from there. As we'll explain in more depth in the next chapter, evacuees often travel farther

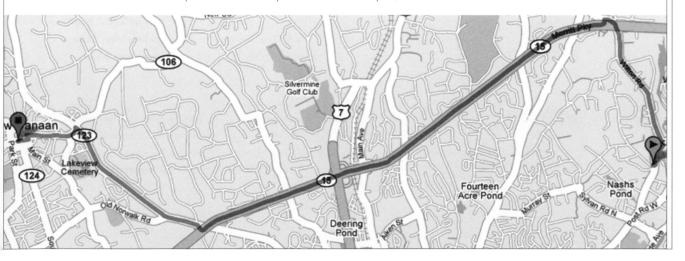

than they have to, which is one reason disasters produce such horrendous traffic jams. Find out the location of some emergency shelters, say, five, 10, and 20 miles from your home. (All cities or counties have emergency management offices that can provide a complete list.) Or if you prefer, think about some hotels that would likely be out of harm's way, and look up the phone numbers to keep with the rest of your supplies. Think about friends or relatives you could stay with, and check with them now to make sure they really wouldn't mind having you live with them for several days or weeks. The point is, bug-out situations are stressful enough without thinking about all these issues for the first time as the NOAA® radio and bullhorns are blaring.

When you send your son or daughter off to college with the usual emergency credit card and lectures about sex, drinking, and grades, don't forget to include a bug-out bag. Colleges are at least as susceptible to disasters as everywhere else, but a bug-out bag with a plane ticket home can make everyone rest a little more easily.

Meals Ready to Eat, or MREs, may seem so survivalist underground, but they really are the perfect disaster food-to-go. Order a mixed assortment from Sopakco (the same folks who supply the military) by clicking on MREs under the Resources tab at yoursurvival.com. And keep two or three days' worth in your car bug-out kit. A box of 12 will run you about $70.

MAINTENANCE

WE PROMISED WE wouldn't turn this into an all-consuming project. If you've made it this far, congratulations! Most of the hard work is done. You still have a few brief chapters to go about what to do immediately before, during, and after a disaster (which we truly hope you never have to put to use). In the meantime, use the next page to mark your calendar or the final side of your Express Planner fold-out card and follow this maintenance schedule.

Maintenance Checklist

Once every few years:
- ✓ Review publicly available disaster sources like flood maps and the county disaster and chemical facility registries.

Once a year:
- ✓ Check the condition of your roof.
- ✓ Change batteries in flashlights, lamps, and radios, and replace spares with a fresh batch.
- ✓ Review and possibly raise limits on insurance policies (unless you have guaranteed replacement cost coverage).
- ✓ Replace all prescription and over-the-counter medications in your emergency medicine kit.
- ✓ Replace food and water in vehicle bug-out box.

Once every six months:
- ✓ Rotate food in disaster supply into everyday cabinets and replace with fresh batch.

Once a season:
- ✓ Change clothes in bug-out bags to more season-appropriate attire.
- ✓ Test to make sure your sump pump is operating properly.

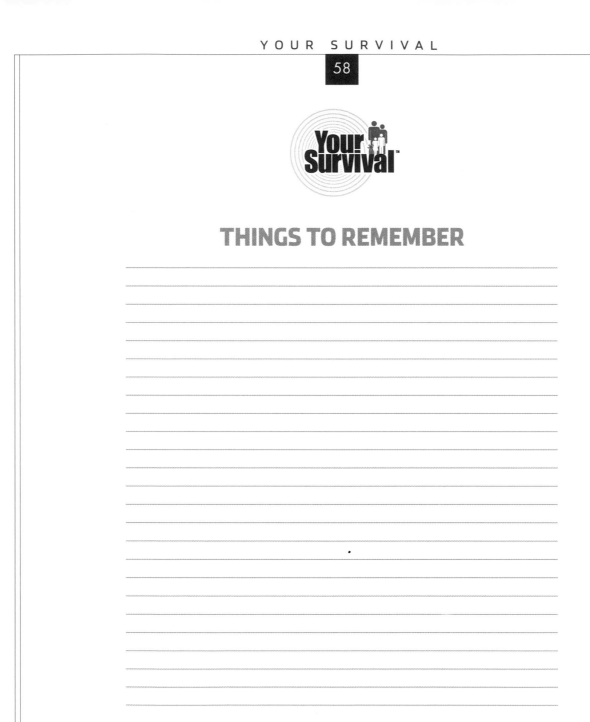

THINGS TO REMEMBER

THINGS TO REMEMBER

"The authorities are never going to tell you not to go, because they don't want the liability."

Chapter 3

STAY OR GO?

In This Chapter

✓ Knowing when to evacuate and when to stay

✓ Speeding up your evacuation trip

✓ Making the best use of the hours before the storm

AS A PSYCHOLOGIST, TIM DONOHOE SHOULD HAVE KNOWN

not to put too much stock in his sense of invulnerability. After evacuating from his Waveland, Mississippi, beachfront home, first for Hurricane Ivan and then for Dennis, and ending up with little more than a few inches of rain each time, the married father of two grown children figured Katrina would be more of the same. "I was all ready to stay," he says. "Then the night before the storm, the police came by and told my wife and I they needed us to write our Social Security numbers on our arms or chests with an indelible marker so they'd be able to identify the bodies afterward. That's when I sat back down with my wife and looked at her and said maybe we oughta rethink this." Donohoe, whose house was indeed completely demolished by the 30-foot surge that crashed into his portion of the coast, was fortunate he got a second chance. Don't press your family's luck. Follow Your Survival's™ safe, reasonable, level-headed approach to evacuation strategy, and everyone under your care should stay safely out of harm's way.

SIX RULES TO LIVE BY

RULE NO. 1: Listen to the Authorities

Virtually every community in this country has some sort of emergency management office. Although they're by no means infallible (and some have better track records than others), you need to listen to what they're saying: When they report that the Weather Service has issued a "watch" for your area, it means to just generally be on alert; a "warning" means no ifs, ands, or buts—whatever onslaught has been predicted for your area is definitely on its way. A "mandatory evacuation" means officials will bear no responsibility if anyone in your family is stranded, hurt, or killed.

RULE NO. 2: Run From Water and Mud

If you're at risk for serious flooding, and storm surges or swollen riverbanks have been predicted for your area, you shouldn't even hesitate—you need to bug out now while you still have time. During Katrina just about the only people who stayed behind in locales like Tim Donohoe's and survived were the insane few who

Lessons Learned

"By our estimates, there are probably a million people in the Houston area who evacuated from Hurricane Rita who had no business being on the roads. People saw New Orleans the week before and they just freaked. But most of Houston is 40 miles or more from the coast! The traffic jams that resulted were a big headache for a lot of people, but it could have been much worse. If that huge tie-up on I-10 had lasted a little longer and the storm hadn't veered off to the east, it could've made for a very scary night out there."

— Mike Lindell, senior scholar with the Texas A&M Hazard Reduction and Recovery Center

happened to be outside and grabbed onto tree limbs. It doesn't matter how well you think your family can swim. Floodwaters behave like no swimming pool or ocean you've ever been in, and are to be avoided at all costs. The same advice goes for mudslides, if not more so. Even in the absence of warnings, if you live in a mudslide-prone area and you've just been through an extended period of saturating rain, and more intense rainfall is forecasted, you should consider vacating immediately.

RULE NO. 3: Hide From Wind

This is the lesser-known corollary to Rule No. 2. High winds, while they can be terrifying to listen to howling around your house, are usually less of a threat than flood. "The authorities are never going to tell you not to go, because they don't want the liability," says Tim Reinhold, vice president for engineering of the insurance industry's Institute for Building and Home Safety. "But for any hurricane up to about a Category 3, if you're not at risk for flooding, you're generally better off staying where you are and hunkering down inside." Of course, this rule depends somewhat on how sturdy your house is, how exacting the building codes are in your area, or what kind of mitigation strategies you

COMMON
MYTHS

"If a hurricane is approaching you should crosshatch your windows with duct tape."

Duct tape has many fine uses in a disaster setting, but, alas, this isn't one of them. According to the Institute for Business and Home Safety's Tim Reinhold, "The only thing the tape might do is stick together some of the pieces into bigger shards when the wind shatters your windows."

"If a tornado is coming, you should open your windows to equalize the pressure."

The pressure drop from a passing tornado is the least of your worries. Far more destructive, says Reinhold, is the sheer force of the 150, 250, or 300 mph wind. Opening windows just increases your risk of getting filleted by broken glass, and wastes precious seconds you could be using to hide somewhere safe.

decided to undertake in Chapter Two. If you don't think your house will fare well, hide at a neighbor's or nearby community shelter.

RULE NO. 4: **Sprint From Tornadoes**
Of course, there's wind and then there's *wind*. While a Category 3 hurricane packs sustained gusts of up to 130 mph, an F5 tornado churns at a speed of 261 mph or more. Nothing short of a safe room can stand up to that. Complicating matters, tornadoes also come with a greater element of surprise than any

Cliff Vaughn of Oklahoma City's Ground Zero Tornado shelters

other natural disaster except earthquakes. By the time a tornado warning has been issued for your area, you have an average of 12 minutes to take cover.

That's why, when you do get more of a heads-up, as occasionally happens with certain very large storm systems, you need to take advantage of it. During the Billion-Dollar Tornado, for instance, most parts of central Oklahoma were warned up to 40 minutes in advance of the funnel clouds' approach. As devastating as the losses were, they could have been much worse if many people hadn't gotten in their cars and driven out of the way.

For those of you who like getting out ahead of the curve, a pair of real-time weather mapping services at <u>yoursurvival.com</u> gives you access to the same data the authorities use to issue their advisories. Under the Resources tab go to <u>Watching the Storm (Hurricanes)</u> for the NOAA® satellite feed that lets you track the paths of hurricanes from the instant they form off the west coast of Africa. Go to <u>Watching the Storm (Severe Weather)</u> for the Doppler radar of every major disturbance in the U.S. (Once you zoom in on your part of the map, click on <u>"reflectivity base loop"</u> to get the images of exactly where it's raining; click on <u>"velocity base loop"</u> to get the winds.) Either makes for a nifty disaster headquarters homepage.

RULE NO. 5: Know Which Way the Wind Is Blowing

PHOTO BY CHERYL EMPEY

The same sort of tracking and evasion maneuvers involved in escaping tornadoes come into play with other disasters like wildfires and chemical clouds. Whether you stay or go often depends on where the hazard is in relation to your house and which direction and how fast it's moving. This brings us back to Rule No.1: Listen carefully to what the authorities are advising people in your particular neighborhood. If the chemical spill occurs on the northeastern edge of town, for example, and the wind is blowing at five miles an hour to the southwest, it may make sense for many residents to get in their cars and start driving perpendicular to the wind. But if your house is just three-quarters of a mile from the cloud, you may be better off staying—and using the 15 minutes you have left to put plastic and duct tape over your windows and vents and convene an emergency family meeting in your containment room.

RULE NO. 6: Don't Play With Fire

The country's leading wildfire watchdog group advises that if a wildfire has been reported in your area, you may have time for some quick fire-evasion techniques. Shut your windows, take down your drapes, and use your hose and extension ladder to spray down your roof and shrubs. You may even want to fill some buckets and place them around the perimeter of your yard in case any embers drift onto your lawn. But the instant you can see the flames or hear the evacuation order blaring down your street, you need to stop playing fireman and bug out.

SHOULD YOU GO OR STAY?

IF YOU GO

Once you get on the move, a few more simple tips can improve the speed—and safety—of your trip.

✓ **THE EARLIER YOU LEAVE THE BETTER.** It's an axiom of evacuation management that the earlier people get on the road, the less likely they are to get stuck in one of those nightmare disaster traffic tie-ups.

✓ **DON'T GO FARTHER THAN YOU HAVE TO.** The longer you're on the road, the more you're just inviting trouble, and the longer it'll take you to return home to check on damage. "I'm always amazed," says Max Mayfield, of the National Hurricane Center, "at how many people who live in the surge zones along the beach here in South Florida drive to Orlando or even Atlanta. I live 10 miles from the beach in Kendall, which is plenty far to drive for most storms. I've often thought I'd like to arrange a deal with some of those people. They could come stay with me here in Kendall, and outside hurricane season I'd get a couple weekends at their condos on the beach."

✓ **DON'T FREELANCE.** Stick to the designated routes publicized on the airways. As FEMA's Ralph Swisher explains, "You may think you know a better way, but all it takes is one downed tree branch or power line you haven't heard about, and you're out of luck."

IF YOU STAY

If you decide to stay put, it's time to get busy.

✓ **TOP OFF YOUR SUPPLIES.** In a disaster like a hurricane or blizzard where you have several hours or more advance warning, you want to put that time to good use rechecking and plugging the gaps in your supplies. Remember, you can almost never have enough propane, batteries, or, especially, water. Buy yourself a couple of clean trash cans and fill them to the brim with water; then buy some clear caulk to create a tight seal around the drains in your bathtubs and fill them up, too.

✓ **BATTEN DOWN THE HATCHES.** Close the fireplace flue and any other vents to the outside. If it's a toxic chemical cloud that's approaching, haul out your plastic and duct tape. If it's a hurricane, bring in your grill, patio furniture, potted plants and anything else that could turn into a missile in high winds. If you've got the simple sheeted-plywood "hurricane shutters" that most people have, now would be the time to put them up. "Believe me," says Pat Jordan of Fort Lauderdale who has ridden out 10 hurricanes, "you don't want to be struggling with those things when the wind is blowing at 80 miles an hour."

✓ **FILL UP YOUR CARS.** If the power goes, it'll probably go at the pumps, too, so now could be your last chance to buy gas for a while.

✓ **LOAD UP ON ICE.** "Rush out and grab as many bags of ice as you can. Or, even better, get those blue plastic ice packs," advises Jordan. Fill up two or three coolers, "and then pack as much as will fit into your freezer," he says. In October 2005, this approach kept the perishables in Jordan's refrigerator cold for about 24 hours and the food in his freezer cold for about three of the 10 days he and the rest of Fort Lauderdale spent without power after Hurricane Wilma.

THINGS TO REMEMBER

THINGS TO REMEMBER

"Utility poles were crashing all around us and the live wires were falling into the water and bursting into flames."

Chapter 4

WEATHERING THE STORM

In This Chapter

✔ Learning what distinguishes a good hiding place

✔ Creating sheltering instructions

✔ Debunking some dubious safety maneuvers

NATIVE OKLAHOMAN STACY STICE HAD BEEN HIDING FROM TORNADOES

in closets and bathrooms her whole life. By May 3, 1999, she was frankly blasé about it. "I didn't even put my shoes on," says the now-35-year-old Norman, Oklahoma, schoolteacher. "I just got in the tub and was, like, I hope this is over soon so I can get back to watching my TV show."

Shortly after the initial warnings, Stice, who had her cell phone with her, was standing at the back door because her father had called a moment earlier to tell her that from where he was watching on TV it looked as if the tornado had passed by her house. Then the phone rang again. "It was my boyfriend-now-husband. He said, 'What are you doing?' I said, 'I'm at the window.' He said, 'Get back in the f——— tub!'

"It wasn't two seconds after I got back in there that my roof blew off. I was just curled up in a little ball and I closed my eyes and prayed to God, 'Please save my life. I'm not ready to go yet.' People always ask, 'Did you hear the freight train?' But I guess the pressure drop of the tornado caused my ear drums to pop. I didn't

Stacey Stice's hiding place, immediately after the tornado passed through.
Note her loofah sponge still hanging from the shower head.

hear anything. All I could do was feel the vibrations of my house being ripped apart. Then the vibrations stopped. I looked up where my roof had been, and the sun was out—and then I saw smoke and smelled gas. And I thought, I'm getting out of here, because I am *not* about to burn up in this house."

May you never have the same opportunity as Stacy Stice to appreciate of the information contained in this brief, harrowing, but vitally important chapter.

THE 30-SECOND GUIDE TO DISASTER PHYSICS

BEFORE YOU CAN decide where to hide in a disaster, it helps to have a rudimentary understanding of physics. It all comes down to the principle of Irresistible Force Meets Immovable Object. Official disaster-proofing strategies are always designed with this idea in mind. For instance, an F5-rated safe room is specifically built to withstand the force of a 15-foot-long 2x4 crashing into it at 100 mph. Hurricane shutters and sturdy soffits are designed to prevent wind from getting inside cracks, where it can fill up your house like a balloon until your roof pops off and your walls blow down. Earthquake bolts and straps are meant to push back against seismic forces trying to shove walls and floors off of foundations.

COMMON MYTHS

"If you're in your car, the safest place to hide from a tornado is underneath an underpass."

Actually, wind speeds up around very large objects, including underpasses. "We've had some really tragic cases out here of people who hid underneath underpasses who were literally ripped out of their loved ones' arms," says the National Severe Storm Laboratory's Kevin Kelleher. Of course, he adds, it's not like any place on the road during a tornado is particularly safe: "I guess, first, I'd try to stay in my car as long as possible; then, second, maybe try to find a ditch and crouch as low to the ground as possible. Although the thought of getting speared by flying boards or glass doesn't make that very attractive either."

But there are also all sorts of other structures in the man-made world that ordinarily have little to do with disasters that can greatly buffet—or amplify—their effects: An underpass can cause the surrounding wind to actually speed up and funnel right into the spot where you're hiding; a bathroom, reinforced with extra support to hold up heavy objects like

bathtubs, might also be just strong enough, like Stice's shower stall, to remain standing after nearly every other inch of your house is ripped apart. Your homework is to identify and separate the truly safe and immovable from the deceptively flimsy and dangerous.

Lessons Learned

"Our block was like the textbook case of everything you should—and shouldn't—do in a tornado. It's a good thing my wife, daughter, and I went to my parents' storm shelter because our house was completely flattened. My sister, who lived three houses from us, was having a dinner party and decided to wait. Six of them ended up squeezing under mattresses in her bathrooms, her roof blew off, and a shock absorber flew in and bruised her leg. But right across the street from our house, another neighbor was trying to hide in a closet with his claustrophobic wife. He kept trying to get her to stay down, and she actually died. When they found her later, her body had blown clear across the yard face first into a tree."

— *Todd Goolsby, 45, Oklahoma City attorney, on the impact of the Billion-Dollar Tornado on 51st and Eric Streets*

YOUR DISASTER-BY-DISASTER DRILL

TORNADOES

✔ It should go without saying, but before hiding, make sure everyone puts his shoes on. Stacy Stice had a hellish time climbing out of the wreckage of her house barefoot. One man who tried to come rescue her mistook a debris-laden swimming pool for solid ground and fell straight into the water.

✔ If you don't have a safe room, your best option, according to FEMA and NOAA, is to hide in the center of your basement. Unfortunately, many of the homes in the parts of the Southwest at greatest risk for tornadoes don't have basements. In that case, the authorities point out, your next best choice is an interior ground-floor tub or shower stall. If all your tubs are on the second floor or next to exposed windows, another choice is an interior ground-floor closet or hallway. Wherever you are, close the door, or try to pull something large and padded like a mattress overtop you. (Of course, all this assumes you live in a house with a permanent foundation. If you live in a trailer home, all bets are off, and you need to evacuate immediately.)

✔ Once the wind stops, you need to get away from the damage as quickly as possible, but if your house isn't too severely demolished you can try to make your

Lessons Learned

"Before I got into the tub I tried to put my cats in their carrying cases to bring in the bathroom with me. But one of my cats ran underneath the middle of the bed. It was the weirdest thing. She'd never hid under there before, and it took me the longest time to get her and finally drag her out. Well, don't you know that underneath the bed was the only other spot besides the bathroom where that cat would've survived. Somehow she knew."

—*Stacy Stice, survivor, Billion-Dollar Tornado*

way to your water heater and gas pipes. If you hear or smell a leak, use your manual gas shut-off wrench to turn off the main gas line, and wait for the gas company to turn it back on. Otherwise, what's left of your house could explode.

✔ Get your kids in the habit of strapping on a bike or football helmet on their way into your designated hiding place.

HURRICANES AND FLOODS

✔ Hurricanes are less likely than tornadoes to flatten your house, but it doesn't take many nails, broken boards, and shards of glass to shred your feet afterward and limit your access to safety. So the shoe advice is the same: Put them on.

✔ The basement would be a good place to hunker down (the below-grade walls are the strongest and most wind-resistant in your house), if it weren't for the fact that water might pour in and drown you. That's why FEMA says you're usually better off riding out the storm in a ground-floor room. During the height of the storm, if you see your doors starting to bow or hear your walls coming apart, get in the tub or shower stall.

✔ You really shouldn't go outside until you're certain the storm is over—regardless of how curious you are to see the eye. "Remember the eye is a

COMMON MYTHS

"The safest place to hide in an earthquake is under a doorway."

This one is a holdover from the early days of California when most homes were made of adobe bricks. Back then, often the only parts of the houses still standing after quakes were the wooden doorframes. But when was the last time you saw an un-reinforced adobe house? In most modern homes the interior doorframes are no sturdier than other parts of the structure and do little to protect you from falling debris.

Ed Rappaport tracks a storm at the National Hurricane Center.

circle, so if you're located on one edge or the other, it can go past you just like that," says the National Hurricane Center's Max Mayfield. "The winds can go from 130 to 0 miles per hour back up to 130 mph within four or five minutes. That's barely enough time to safely poke your head out." Better to track the storm with your radio or battery-operated TV, and stay put until you get the official word.

✔ If you're out on the road and come across a flood, do whatever you can to steer clear of it. Water weighs 62 pounds per cubic foot, so it doesn't take a lot of it to sweep you away. Just four inches of rapidly moving water can be enough to knock most people off their feet; 12 inches can carry away your car.

EARTHQUAKES

✔ If an earthquake hits at night when you're sleeping, according to the U.S. Geological Survey's David Applegate, the best thing you can do is roll out of bed (literally) and either slide under or lie close to the frame where it can shield you from falling debris. During the daytime, depending on where you are in your house, he adds, the safest spot is either under a sturdy table or by a windowless load-bearing exterior wall. Press your back flat against the wall or crawl under the table and hold onto one table leg to keep it from turning over, and cover your head.

✔ The most common injury from earthquakes is cut feet from broken glass. That's why past quake victims, like L.A. accountant Mitchell Freedman, always ("even if I'm loaded on margaritas") tuck a pair of shoes under their beds at night.

✔ After your shoes are on, you may be able to check your water heater and pipes for the smell and sound of gas. If you suspect you have a leak, use your manual gas shut-off wrench to turn off the main gas line.

✔ If you're outdoors, advises the USGS, try to move into a clear area and get into a crouch with your hands over your head. Avoid bridges, overpasses,

COMMON MYTHS

"You should run uphill from a landslide."

It's unclear how this one got started. One possibility is that the landslide areas of California tend to overlap somewhat with the areas subject to tsunami warnings and you are supposed to run uphill from a tsunami. At any rate, the advice makes absolutely no sense for landslides. At least if you run downhill, says USGS landslide specialist Paula Gori, you have a head start on the structures and debris coming down from further up the slope. Mainly, she says, you just want to stay alert, pick the downhill direction that looks most solid, and drive or run that way as fast as you can.

shattered glass from high-rises, power lines, or anything else that could fall on top of you. If you're in the car, pull over, stop, and set the parking brake.

✓ Try not to get too wigged out by the aftershocks. Nearly every major earthquake has them—sometimes for just a day or two, sometimes for months. Each time you feel another one coming on, follow the same drill as above. There's always a chance that the earthquake was just a prelude and the "aftershock" is the real thing.

CHEMICAL CLOUDS

✓ On your way into your containment room, grab your watch and a radio tuned to the news, and keep close tabs on both. Because of the risk of asphyxiation from carbon dioxide buildup, FEMA emphasizes that even with 10 feet of floor space per person you need to limit your amount of time inside the room to five hours.

LANDSLIDES

✓ Of all the things that go bump in the night, if you ever hear loud popping and cracking sounds, and you live on or near a steep hillside prone to landslides, do NOT just chalk it up to rambunctious raccoons. "The popping is from pipes

Lessons Learned

"We got away from the house out in the street, but then the whole landscape started sliding in our direction. Houses were coming down toward us. The street and sidewalks were flooding because of all the broken water mains. Utility poles were crashing all around us and the live wires were falling into the water and exploding and bursting into flames. Ten of us crammed into my neighbor's truck and tried to drive away. We made it about 30 seconds before the whole street—including our truck— just dropped 75 feet. At that point, the only thing I could think to say was, 'Are you kidding me?'"

– Jill Lockhart, 38, who escaped with her two toddlers from the 2005 Laguna Beach landslide while her husband Bobby was out of town

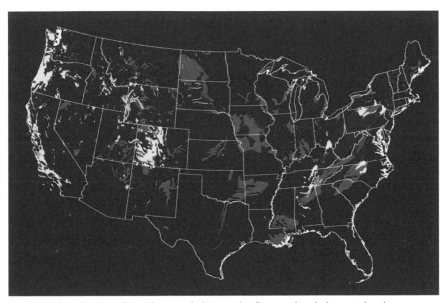

Landslide risk in the U.S.: Red areas have very high potential, yellow areas have high potential, and green areas have moderate potential. Landslides can and do occur in the black areas, but the potential is low.

bursting. The cracking is from the wood in your house ripping apart," says Jill Lockhart, a photography stylist, who used these telltale sounds as her signal to wake her 2- and 4-year-olds and safely flee the 2005 Laguna Beach Landslide

HEAT WAVES

✓ The advice may seem obvious, but then why do an average of 170 people die each year in heat waves? So FEMA's guidelines warrant repeating: Drink plenty of fluids, avoid strenuous work during the warmest parts of the day, and stick close to air conditioning. If anyone starts experiencing the symptoms of heat exhaustion (profuse sweating, pale or flushed skin color, and dizziness, nausea, or headaches), get the person into a cool environment and slowly hydrate with a half glass of water every 15 minutes; with heat stroke (high body temperature, red skin, shallow breathing, and rapid, weak pulse), do the same and call 911 immediately. And if you know of seniors in an un-air-conditioned home or apartment, get them out of there—before they add to the statistics.

WINTER STORMS

✔ If your regular heating system goes out, and you're forced to use your back-up, be mindful of proper venting. The propane heater we recommend, the Mr. Heater™ "Portable Buddy," (p.31) has an automatic low-oxygen shut-off system that will prevent carbon monoxide poisoning. In a standard room open to the rest of the house, you can use it without any additional precautions. You may decide, however, that it's more efficient to close the door to one room and heat up a small contained area, in which case you'll want to crack one window a quarter of an inch.

✔ Further conserve heat by shutting off unneeded rooms, nailing up blankets over your windows at night—and eating! Food provides the body with energy to help it produce its own heat.

✔ If you must venture out, wear multiple layers of loose-fitting, lightweight warm clothing, rather than one heavy layer. Cover your head and mouth, and opt for mittens over gloves.

✔ Try to stay off the roads—70 percent of all winter storm deaths occur in automobiles. If you do end up getting stranded on a remote roadway, tie a piece of cloth to the antennae and then stay inside the car and wait for help. Run the engine and heater about 10 minutes every hour, cracking the window to avoid carbon monoxide poisoning. Look for signs of frostbite (loss of feeling and whitening of extremities). If immediate medical help isn't available, slowly re-warm the affected areas. Hypothermia (uncontrollable shivering, memory loss, disorientation, apparent exhaustion) should be addressed by using anything at your disposal—blankets, car mats, or your own body—to warm the person's core first. This is critical, because warming the extremities first can cause cold blood to rush to the heart and cause a heart attack.

✔ Don't eat snow! While it's important to stay hydrated, you need to melt it first; otherwise, it'll just lower your body temperature.

WILDFIRES

✔ There's never a good reason to choose to stay and weather a fire, but if your planning has gone awry and you're trapped by a wildfire, do NOT try to outrun it. Ironically, you're better off inside your house than out. Most wildfires will pass by your house before they burn it down. Then, as soon as the fire passes, check your roof and attic for sparks, and douse with whatever water you have on hand.

✔ Similarly, if you get trapped on the road, DON'T leave your car. Roll up your windows and close the air vents. Drive slowly with your headlights on. If you have to stop, get on the floor and cover up with a coat or the car mats until the fire

What you should do if you're threatened by a wildfire is completely different from the advice for a regular house fire. During a wildfire, you are better inside your house than out. But if there is a fire in your house, then you just want to get out as soon as possible. Check the heat of a closed door before exiting a room; if it's hot and a window exit is available, use that instead. Stay low or crawl as you exit the building because the air is clearer and cooler near the floor.

passes. Sparks may enter the vehicle, air currents may rock the car, and the temperature inside may soar, but metal gas tanks rarely explode.

✔ If you're trapped in the open, seek some sort of ditch or natural depression with a low amount of brush. A road cut on the uphill side of a road would be ideal. Clear as much fuel as you can with the time you have left, then lie face down and cover yourself with anything that might shield you from the fire until it passes.

✔ And if your clothes ever catch fire, drop and roll until the flames are extinguished. Running only makes fire burn faster.

THINGS TO REMEMBER

THINGS TO REMEMBER

"It was like I was watching somebody else. Like I was watching someone else's house that had burned down."

Chapter 5

IMMEDIATE AFTERMATH

In This Chapter

✔ Making supplies last

✔ Stop-gap repairs and getting your insurer on the case

✔ Grieving and recognizing signs of post-traumatic stress

"THERE'S NO SCRIPT FOR THIS.

No book you can order on eBay®." When Kathy Hebert said this she was referring to what it's like to look up one day and find half your house missing, all your friends moved away, and half the city where your family has lived since the 1700s leveled by a hurricane. But she could have also been talking about tapping your water heater so your family doesn't go thirsty, sleeping five to a hotel room as you figure out where you're going to live for the next six months, dickering with your insurance carrier, and the dozens of other strange, traumatic, bewildering challenges that people all across the country face every year in the immediate days and weeks after a disaster. Hebert is right, there is no script for this part. However, hearing how others got through it, rehearsing in your mind how you might react to the circumstances you'll face, and learning about the resources that are available to you can help.

PRACTICALITIES FIRST

YOUR COPING STRATEGIES for the first few days will vary greatly, depending on how much damage your property sustained, whether you were forced to evacuate, or are now stranded at home, cut off from power and other basic services. If you had to bug out, presumably you're now some-place safe and (relatively) comfortable, and the primary issue you need to deal with is your anxiety over the condition of your house. Be patient, and try to remember that whatever damage there is has likely already been done, and returning home before the area is re-secured won't accomplish anything—except possibly putting your family in danger. If you hunkered down and are contending with extended utility outages, your most immediate concerns have to do with coming up with new card games and trying not to think about how long it's been since anyone has showered.

"You just have to shift into what I call 'cowboy mode,'" says veteran hurricane survivor Pat Jordan. "You don't want to use up your water on bathing, so you wear as little as possible and try not to move around too much. Every morning you heat up your coffee in your little metal coffee pot, dinner is usually either baked beans or spaghetti, and you play a lot of cards. Some people down here also drink a lot, which seems to help." Beyond that advice, it's probably worth mentioning just a few more pointers in four crucial areas.

MANAGING YOUR WATER SUPPLY

MOST PEOPLE DON'T realize how much liquid they take in during the course of an ordinary day via juices, sodas, fruit, vegetables, and various prepared foods. But in a "cowboy-mode" situation, where most of what you eat is either dried or canned, you can easily become dehydrated. Every family member should be drinking at least eight glasses of water a day. That's in addition to the water you'll be using to fix food and coffee. At that rate (unless you went in for 55-gallon water drums), you could soon find yourself running low, but there are some measures you can take to stretch your supply.

✔ **COLLECT RAINWATER** On day one of the crisis, you can put out a tarp to collect rain and dew water. Create a kind of inverted tent by tying each corner to a tree or some sort of pole or piece of lawn furniture. As the water collects at the bottom, either transfer the water to pots and heat over a grill to boil off microbes, or run through your water purifier.

✔ **TAP YOUR WATER HEATER** All water heaters have a clean-out valve at the bottom. Attach a hose to it and you can siphon out 30 or more gallons of perfectly potable water. The first few gallons may have sediment in them. Just wait until that runs clear. Then fill up as many empty water jugs as you think you'll need that day, and shut the valve back off.

✔ **FLUSHING** Even without running water, you can flush your toilet if you fill the tank. We suggest you use the water that you filled your trash cans and tubs with for this purpose. About two and a half gallons per flush should do it—and try to ration your flushes as best you can.

GETTING HELP FROM THE RED CROSS

OF ALL THE CHARITABLE and governmental disaster relief agencies, the Red Cross specializes, as it likes to say, in "the first three days." Services can range from putting you up in a hotel or one of its own shelters to providing a stipend for meals or extra changes of clothes. Through its role in something

Lessons
Learned

"After we evacuated to Houston, we had a hard time with our younger children complaining about wanting to go home. They saw the pictures on TV of people moving around the French Quarter, and they couldn't understand what was going on. My kids hadn't been in the Superdome or gone through the flooding. To them, it was almost like a vacation: They got to live in a hotel room and there was no school. But now they wanted to go home. We kept trying to explain to them why we couldn't. They still didn't get it. Kids, especially young kids, only understand what they see right in front of them. So, finally, on one of our trips back we decided to take them with us. They stopped complaining after that."

— *Deborah Irabor, whose home overlooking Lake
Pontchartrain was devastated by Hurricane Katrina*

called the National Voluntary Organizations Active in Disaster (NVOAD) the organization is also a great clearinghouse for other slightly longer-term or more specialized resources, from the Next of Kin Registry (1-800-915-5413) that can help find lost loved ones to the credit-card hotlines for Discover (1-800-DIS-COVER) and Mastercard (1-800-MC-ASSIST) that can help with payment relief to Catholic Charities and the Salvation Army.

In a highly localized disaster like the flooding of a neighborhood, the Red Cross will usually come find you, but if you need to find them you should make your way to the nearest FEMA or other governmental command center (see below) and just look for the big red cross or a representative who can point you in the right direction. (Depending on space, sometimes the Red Cross will set up in the same facility as the governmental authorities, and sometimes in a nearby school or public building.) If you have access to a phone or the Internet, you can also contact your local Red Cross chapter.

GETTING HELP FROM FEMA

FOR ALL THE CRITICISM FEMA has come under—much of it deserved—the agency is still an important resource at your disposal. If you live in an official presidentially declared **Disaster Zone** and your home has been totalled and you have limited insurance coverage, you could be eligible for a housing allowance for up to 18 months. Call 1-800-621-FEMA or talk to the representatives at any FEMA

We've included a couple of key Red Cross links under the resources tab at yoursurvival.com. To find the Red Cross chapter in your area go to Red Cross Chapters. For the most useful list of Red Cross NOVAD partner organizations (on the Red Cross's own website, the lis is actually buried under the hurricane section) go to Red Cross Partners.

Disaster Recovery Center. Within several days of the disaster, the center locations should be broadcast in fliers and on radio and TV. Or check the bulletin board at Your Survival List at yoursurvival.com.

FEMA is also your premier source for roof tarps. In major disasters involving a lot of wind damage, you can usually get free "FEMA blue" tarps to keep the elements out of your house while you wait on insurance adjusters and contractors. Or you can have the U.S. Army Corps of Engineers install sheets of a slightly more durable plastic material (in a similar shade of blue). Get the tarps at your local FEMA Recovery Center; sign up for the hard plastic sheeting at the same center or by calling 1-800-ROOFBLU.

NOTIFYING YOUR INSURANCE COMPANY

ASSUMING YOU DO have proper coverage, as soon as your phone service returns you need to call your insurance company and start your claim. Insurers are like deli counters: They work on a first-come, first-served basis. So the sooner they have a claim number for you, the sooner they can get the ball rolling to get you your money.

　　If you did a thorough job of inventorying your possessions and evaluating your policies, you probably don't have anything to worry about right now. But you still might meet with some resistance from the other side of the counter. In the next chapter, we'll go into more detail about what you should do if you have a dispute with your insurer. In the meantime, it's best not to contribute to any delays.

THE STAGES OF DISASTER GRIEF

O **FTEN THE MOST** difficult part of a disaster's aftermath isn't the actual lack of showers, arguments with your insurance company, or strategizing about how to put your house back together, but the powerful emotions these things stir in us. "Disasters literally knock the ground out from underneath our feet," says Christine Curci, Ph.D., a Maine-based mental health specialist who works with Susan Briggs on the East Coast International Medical Surgical Response Team. "They knock us out of psychological balance. People have to find a way to restore that balance, and that takes time."

Everyone reacts to a major disaster somewhat differently. But there are patterns, and recognizing those patterns can help you realize that whatever shifting, chaotic feelings you're experiencing are probably completely normal. The first emotion almost every disaster victim experiences is shock. Roberta Winston, a 45-year-old San Diego attorney and mother of three, describes her reaction when she first learned the fate of her house after the famous 2003 Scripps Ranch Wildfire. She had evacuated with her family to her mother's house across town and was watching the fire on TV when she noticed that a camera on the scene had focused on her house. The only part of her home she could see on the screen was the stucco archway around her front door; a spigot, which had somehow turned on and was spraying water onto her front stoop; and just one tiny corner of her garage—which she could see, had caught fire. "I figured, 'Huh, that's not so bad,'" she recalls. "I mean, if the whole house was in flames, they would have pulled back for a more dramatic shot, right?" All afternoon, the TV station kept returning to that same shot, which continued to give Winston

hope. Finally, late in the day, the shot came on again, and this time the camera pulled back. That's when Winston saw: the archway, the spraying spigot, the smoldering corner of the garage was all that was left of her house. "It was just the strangest feeling," she says. "It was like I was watching somebody else. Like I was watching the news and saw someone else's house that had just burned to the ground."

Winston then had another typical disaster reaction: a torrent of tears and anger, the classic feelings of "Why me?" At that point, says Curci, "some people will just fall apart and be unable to function for days or even weeks. But you don't see that too much. What you mainly see is an amazing amount of resilience." High-functioning, take-charge types, especially, tend to shift quickly out of feeling-sorry-for-themselves into "survival mode," as Curci calls it, as they attempt to control as much of the situation as they can. By the next morning, in fact, Winston had already filed her claim with her insurance company and talked to a house builder she and her husband knew from their synagogue. Within a week she'd found her family comfortable temporary quarters and had started to replace her children's favorite toys and stuffed animals. Within three months, her claim had been processed, the blueprints finished, and ground was being broken on her new house.

Lessons Learned

"During Mardi Gras, a woman came into the clinic with her husband and two kids. It was their first day back in the city. They had a FEMA trailer, but it didn't have utilities, so they'd decided to stay in the un-destroyed upstairs of their house. And that morning they had gotten in a car accident. The woman was just beside herself. 'What am I going to do?' she said. 'My stress is already off the charts.' So we strategized a little, and then I asked her, 'So, what about you?' That's when she told me it was going to be really hard the next few mornings to wake up and not have a kitchen to fix herself a cup of tea in. I said, 'Do you have enough money for a hot plate? Good, we're going to put your husband to work finding you a hot plate so you can fix yourself tea.' She seemed better after that."

— *Christine Curci, Hurricane Katrina grief counselor*

But right at about the four- or five-month mark, Winston hit a kind of emotional wall. "I started feeling really tired out by it all," she says. She began to have difficulty sleeping, and increasingly found herself snapping at her husband and kids, and kept "waiting for the other shoe to drop," as she wondered what tragedy awaited her family next.

"It doesn't matter how 'together' you are," says Curci, "or how well your efforts are paying off. That initial imbalance I was talking about is eventually going to catch up with you. Disasters alter our view of the world. They change what we thought we knew. This sense we have of ourselves of not being vulnerable to these sorts of things suddenly no longer holds. So, until you come up with a new way of looking at the world that takes that into account, you're going to be stuck, and not be able to truly move on."

GETTING UNSTUCK

IF (OR, MORE LIKELY, when) you get stuck during the emotional processing of a disaster, you need to recognize the signs and seek help. Many victims find that talking to close friends, family, or their pastor helps. But if you're so depressed you can't get out of bed or carry on with the work still left to be done, you need to talk to get a professional referral. Talk to your physician or local church-affiliated counseling agency. Or contact the National Mental Health Association affiliate in your area.

Mainly, though, you need to give yourself time, and recognize that disasters present an opportunity: an opportunity for emotional growth. "We in this country tend to believe we can control everything," says Curci. "Other cultures, I think, are more realistic in that respect. They know there are forces far greater than us, and that the best we can do is to prepare and then just trust in ourselves. Going through a disaster can teach you a new way of going through the

Billion-Dollar Tornado survivor Leslie Bryant

world that, I'd argue, is more in tune with the way things really were all along. And if you can get to that point you've got a chance to be a happier, stronger person all around." For Roberta Winston, the light bulb finally came on during a phone conversation with her sister, who, coincidentally, is a grief counselor based in Florida. "I kept having trouble getting past wondering about the next bad thing that was going to happen to us," Winston says. "Then I finally decided, Well, if something else happens, we'll just deal with that, too."

Among mental health organizations, the National Mental Health Association has taken the lead in helping its members be more attuned to the special needs of disaster victims. Go to the NHMA Database under the resources tab at yoursurvival.com to find the phone number of your local affiliate. Then just call the office and a trained staffer will help match you with a therapist experienced at working through these sorts of issues.

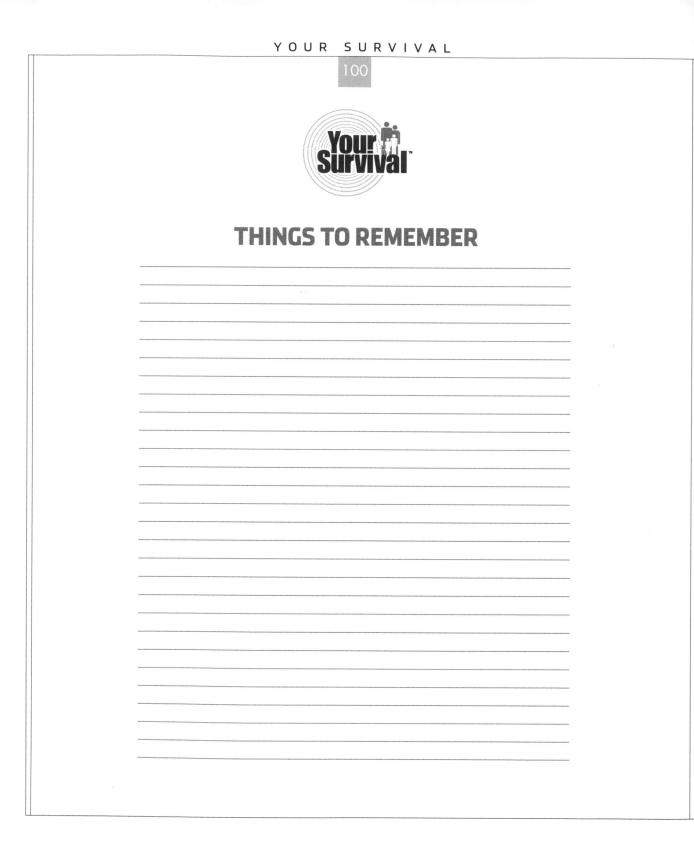

THINGS TO REMEMBER

THINGS TO REMEMBER

"My husband had a feeling we needed a
lawyer, and I was like, 'No, just give it time.
He seems like a nice guy.'"

ALLSTATE PAID $10,113.34
ON THIS HOUSE
FOR STORM DAMAGE

Chapter 6

REBUILDING

In This Chapter

✓ Leveling the playing field with your
  insurance and mortgage companies

✓ Doing your contractor due-diligence

✓ Working the tax and government angles

FOR SOME PEOPLE, REBUILDING IS LIKE A SECOND DISASTER:

fights with insurance companies, unscrupulous contractors, AWOL building inspectors, government "relief" programs ensnarled in miles and miles of red tape. "And then as if things weren't bad enough," says Katrina victim Kathy Hebert, "we got a notice from the IRS. We put in our un-reimbursed damages as a tax deduction, as you're encouraged to do, and now we're getting audited! Isn't that great? I have half a house and I'm out about $200,000, and now I'm getting audited!"

We're not going to sugarcoat the situation for you: Putting your life back together after a major disaster is hard, time-consuming, and exhausting work. But if you've paid careful attention up until now, and use the expert insider's advice in this chapter to side-step some of the common pitfalls that trap people like Kathy Hebert, you can limit the disasters to just the one.

DOUBLECHECK YOUR MENTAL STATE

AS WE SAID IN the previous chapter, it can take many months to fully process the emotional fallout of a disaster—or sometimes even to recognize that that's what's going on. As you move forward with the practicalities of putting your life back together you'll want to stay on the lookout for the warning signs of lingering post-traumatic stress: increasing irritability or snappishness; unexplained fatigue; loss of appetite; trouble sleeping or going about your regular routine. If these describe you or someone close to you, don't try to "tough it out." Any of the resources described on page 98 can help you demystify the process of finding a qualified counseling help. And if you're ever so despondent that you're actually afraid of what you might do next, call 1-800-273-TALK. Trained National Mental Health Association counselors are on-call to make sure you don't do anything too rash, and you give yourself time to heal.

STAYING ON YOUR INSURER

THE INSURANCE industry isn't going to like this, but when it comes to dealing with your insurer we want you to adopt the old motto of the X-Files® agent Mulder: "Trust no  one." As we said in the first chapter, it's not that insurance companies are evil; to the contrary, they've paid out close to $100 billion in disaster-related claims over the past couple of years. If it wasn't for the insurance industry post-Katrina, this country would be in dire straits right about now. And yet, on an individual case basis, one of the ways they stay in business is by sometimes adopting a very hard-nosed attitude toward that contract you signed with them those many months or years ago. It's like any business transaction, says Ken Strauss, a Miami accountant who focuses on disaster-related issues and has advised numerous clients on dealing with insurers: "If they think you're a sophisticated and well-represented person, you may have an easier time of it."

With that in mind, Strauss and other leading insurance advisors offer these tips on how to present yourself as the sort of tough, sophisticated SOB (Survivor Or Bust) that any insurance company would want to try to keep happy:

✔ **HIRE YOUR OWN EXPERT.** Usually within a few weeks after you put in your claim an insurance adjustor will come to your house to assess the damages. After major disasters the big companies will fly in hundreds of such people from across the country (known in the industry as "storm troopers"), many of them unfamiliar with local building costs and customs. The adjustor will walk through your house, punching information into a handheld computer pre-programmed with certain standardized formulas for estimating repair costs. He'll note that your living room windows are blown out, for example, and punch in "four living room windows" and one number will pop up; then he'll see the gaping hole in your bedroom ceiling and punch in "9 x 15 sheet of drywall"

Lessons Learned

"I tell people who ask what it looked like to try to imagine someone taking two dump trucks worth of mud and emptying it into your house. Then filling your house with water, and then shaking it up and down a couple times. Then they let all that muddy water sit for two weeks, festering. So when that foul water is finally pumped out, and you walk into your house and pick up your kitchen table, it actually falls apart in your hands. And you look at your refrigerator and it's somehow been wedged in between the counter and the wall, and you wonder, 'How the hell did that get in there?'"

—Joe Gallodoro, St. Bernard Parish, Louisiana

and another number will pop up. Then when he's done, he'll tabulate the results, and offer to write you a check, sometimes right on the spot. It's likely to be a big check. Maybe bigger than anyone has ever offered to write you before. Don't let yourself be too impressed. There's a chance it's not big enough.

The only way you can tell for certain if it's enough is to have a reputable contractor walk through the site and tell you whether he believes he can do the job for that amount. Now, frequently after a disaster, that will be impossible because you can't find a contractor to give you the time of day. That's when you need to go back to your insurer and ask how the company handles filing

It may sound obvious, but take 30 seconds and get the adjustor's name and phone number, advises Joe Gallodoro of the Professional Insurance Agents of Louisiana. "I can't tell you how many people forget. Then they call me three months later to check on the status of their claim and it takes me two weeks just to find out who to check with."

a supplemental claim, which you will need to do if the job ends up costing more than they estimated. You should also check with the state insurance commissioner. Some states, like Florida, have well-organized insurance mediation programs set up specifically to deal with jobs that run over their original cost adjustments. But if you don't like the answers you're receiving on those fronts, then you can hire an expert, known as a "public adjustor," to counter the insurance company's offer with a detailed estimate of your own. The insurance commissioner's office, accountants, and independent insurance agents can all help with referrals; public adjustors usually charge a flat fee of around $300.

✓ **DON'T ACCEPT THE FIRST ANSWER.** "It's true what they say: The squeaky wheel gets the grease," says Joe Gallodoro, president of the New Orleans chapter of the Professional Insurance Agents of Louisiana. Gallodoro gives a perfect example of what he's talking about—his own. In addition to the flood damage to his house, for which he's been paid up to the limit of his flood insurance policy, his roof also blew off. As insurers often do, Allstate wrote him a check for the depreciated value of his roof, $4,000, and informed him that after he had a new one installed he could send them the receipt and they would reimburse him for the additional $8,000 it's estimated to cost. "They said that's their official procedure. But I don't care, I wrote them a letter saying, 'With everything else going on, I shouldn't have to pay $8,000 out of my own pocket just to put a roof back on my house. I need you to pay me that money right now."

**Lessons
Learned**

"Afterward, the thing I had the hardest time with wasn't the fact that I had been through a tornado. It was how nice people were. I kept wondering, Why are all these people being so nice to me? I mean, people gave me money. A woman at school lent me her car. My insurance company was awesome. Since then, whenever I hear of someone who's been through something like this, I make sure to give. It's like that movie: *Pay It Forward*."

— *Stacy Stice, Billion-Dollar Tornado survivor*

✔ IF YOU THINK YOU NEED A LAWYER, YOU PROBABLY DO.

Hiring a lawyer is expensive and generally to be avoided. It certainly wasn't something Deborah Irabor even considered for the longest time. "At first, it seemed like everything was going along smoothly. An adjustor came out and said, 'Yeah, it looks like you have a total loss here.' Then a few weeks later a new adjustor came out and started questioning everything, and trying to get us to pass it off on our flood insurance policy. He was saying, 'Well, how do know this water damage was from the wind and rain and not flood?' and 'Maybe we can just cut in some new drywall and patch over this spot here.' My husband had a feeling right then that we should get a lawyer, and I was, like, 'No, just give it time. He seems like a nice guy.'" Six months later, after the Irabors continued to cool their heels in Houston with little movement on their claim, they finally hired a lawyer. "In retrospect I wish we'd done it way back in the beginning," Deborah says. As a general rule, you can usually tell if your insurer is preparing for a fight. If they are, delaying the inevitable frequently only drags out the pain.

APPLYING FOR FEMA ASSISTANCE

AS PART OF the federal aid for presidentially declared Disaster Zones, the Federal Emergency Management Agency has funds set aside to help people without insurance, with too little insurance, or with an insurance company that is either delaying on contesting the payment of its claim. If a Disaster Zone has been declared in your area and you think you may be eligible, pick up an application form along with a copy of "Help After a Disaster: Applicant's Guide to the Individuals and Households Program" at any FEMA Recovery Center.

FEMA's aid essentially falls into two main categories. Its first, and primary, area of responsibility is to reimburse you for temporary living expenses, such as rent and meals, or to actually provide such housing in the form of a trailer—

the much-maligned white metal one-bedroom "FEMA trailers," which are generally to be avoided. Depending on which market you live in, the agency usually caps its cash grants at $27,000 per family.

FEMA may also provide some money to repair the damages to your home and possessions. Its assistance in this area, though, is only intended to fill in the gaps left by another important government resource, known as the Small Business Administration (SBA) Disaster Loan Program (see page 115). But—and this important—private homeowners and renters cannot apply for an SBA disaster loan until they register with FEMA. (To show how seriously the agencies take this requirement, the SBA's own website doesn't even mention the program.) After you file your FEMA application, FEMA will refer your case to the SBA and you'll receive an SBA loan application in the mail. Alternatively, after you file, you can pick up a copy of the SBA loan application at a FEMA Recovery Center or by calling 1-800-659-2955.

Yoursurvival.com makes a concerted effort to guide you through the maze of government and relief agency websites that may be able to help your family get back on its feet. Under the resources tab you'll find the FEMA Application Form that's such a critical first step for getting into the FEMA and Small Business Association relief pipeline. There are also links to FEMA's list of Other Government Agencies That Can Help and its list of Below-Market Temporary Housing options in your area. Families in especially dire need may try to Apply for a Habitat for Humanity Home or Apply for Extreme Makeover: Home Edition, the popular ABC reality series. Just be aware that Habitat's resources are limited and the organization requires a significant contribution of sweat equity, and Extreme Makeover helps just 24 families a year.

DEALING WITH YOUR MORTGAGE COMPANY

IF YOU WERE SEVERELY underinsured, there may not be much you can do to keep your mortgage company from forcing you to use your settlement to pay off your mortgage. It all depends on how interest rates have behaved since you took out the loan. If the rates have gone up a lot, it doesn't matter if you argue until you're blue in the face—your mortgage company is probably going to exercise its right to call in the old, below-market note. If, on the other hand, interest rates have dropped, you may find your lender acting uncharacteristically generous. Sure, you can keep your insurance money, they may say. And why don't you let us loan you another $100,000 at the same terms so you can finish the job. Don't do it! Under those circumstances, you'd actually be better off using your settlement to pay off your mortgage, and starting over with a 120-day construction loan that converts to a fresh mortgage at today's lower rates.

HIRING A CONTRACTOR

IF DEALING WITH insurance and mortgage companies after a disaster can be frustrating, dealing with the building trades can drive a person to complete distraction. Kathy Hebert describes what happened after waiting three months for someone from the Jefferson Parish building department to come inspect the new wiring in her first floor so she could start putting walls back up: "I was on the phone with one guy, and he was telling me it was going to be another few weeks on top of the 12 weeks I had already waited, and I just started crying. He finally said, 'Okay lady, don't worry about it, I'm going to sign off on it from here. Go ahead and cover your walls.'"

The contracting field, a loosely organized, understaffed, chaotic industry under ordinary circumstances, becomes a free-for-all in the wake of a major disaster. The best contractors immediately become overwhelmed by too much work; inspectors get backlogged; fly-by-night firms converge on the area from out of state; and a lot of otherwise savvy homeowners end up paying a lot more for repairs than they should.

Florida, which has as much experience as any state with rebuilding from disasters, started something several years ago called the Disaster Contractors Network to attempt to deal with some of these issues. Douglas Buck, the Florida Homebuilders' Association government liaison who was instrumental in founding the DCN, offers the following handful of simple tips borne of, as he says, "way too much practice."

✔ **START WHEN YOU'RE READY.** If you nab a terrific contractor before prices shoot up, great. Otherwise, especially if you're not under immediate pressure from your mortgage company, try not to let yourself get rushed into bad decisions. If you can put up with the cramped temporary quarters, dust, and drip buckets, you're often better off trying to delay construction until the market settles down a bit.

✓ **GET COMPETITIVE BIDS.** In a non-disaster, they say you're always supposed to get three bids. That may be nearly impossible post-disaster, but get at least two bids, even if the contractors insist on being paid a couple of hundred dollars each to draw up the estimates. Then just insist that the firm you hire deducts its fee off the final bill.

✓ **CHECK WITH YOUR STATE'S LICENSING BOARD.** You may need to hire a contractor you've never heard of before. That's okay, but ask to speak to past clients, and in states that license contractors, check with the licensing board to confirm that the contractor's license is in good standing; if the company is from out of state, check with the licensing board in its home state.

✓ **GET A SIGNED CONTRACT.** The contractor should provide one. If he doesn't have one, your local building department should be able to direct you to where you can find a standard contract for your state. (Or another contractor may even let you use one of his.) "And please," says Buck, "have the contractor fill out the draw schedule. Any contractor who asks you to put 90 percent upfront, or asks you to pay for materials is not a contractor you want to be dealing with." A reasonable fee schedule, Buck says, would require 20 percent up front, then one to three more installments, depending on the scope and length of the project.

✓ **MAKE SURE THE CONTRACTOR ARRANGES FOR ALL NECESSARY PERMITS AND PICKS THEM UP HIMSELF.** Check with your building department to find out which permits are required and then see that your contractor gets them and locks in a spot in the building inspector queue at least roughly corresponding to when various parts of the job are done. If he asks you to pick up the permits, that's a bad sign. It might mean he's illegally operating without a license and is afraid of getting caught.

GETTING THE IRS TO HELP

MOST DISASTER VICTIMS don't realize that there are tax provisions specifically designed to help them deal with insurance shortfalls and mortgage and cash flow headaches. According to the federal tax code, anyone who lives in an official Disaster Zone can withdraw money from their 401k without any tax penalties, as long as it's paid back within 60 days.

Furthermore, those same people can file an amended tax return to reflect the un-reimbursed damages to their property. For example, say your house was worth $400,000 and it's been completely demolished; your insurance company reimburses you $100,000, and the lot in its current state is worth about another $100,000. You now have a $200,000 loss that you can deduct from your prior year's income and for which you're entitled to a refund. What if you didn't make $200,000? It doesn't matter. You can take the loss for two more previous years until you max out the deduction. For most tax brackets, a family in this situation would receive a check from the IRS in the neighborhood of $40,000.

But, as Kathy Hebert found out, this aspect of the rebuilding process has its own perils. "The difficulty is in determining what the real loss in value is," explains Ken Abney, a New Orleans accountant who has been dealing with this issue on an almost daily basis. "Are you sure that's all you're getting from the insurance company? And is the current value of the property what your appraiser says it is or what a speculator just paid for a property down the street? In New Orleans the IRS just came out with some cost indexes to help us figure it out."

No one should try to file an amended return without the advice of an accountant. If you don't have an accountant and need one, whether for help filing an amended return or for any other post-disaster financial issue, go to <u>Find an Accountant</u> under the Resources tab at <u>yoursurvival.com,</u> which will link you to the referral network run by the American Institute of Certified Public Accountants. After major disasters, the AICPA also establishes phone banks and sets up booths in Red Cross centers to dispense free advice. Look for details at Your Survival List at <u>yoursurvival.com.</u>

SOLVING THE GOVERMENT LOAN PUZZLE

AS INDICATED EARLIER, there is one more financial resource available—or at least theoretically available—to many disaster victims: a low-interest loan from the Small Business Administration. Post-Katrina press reports have been highly critical of the SBA. The paperwork is reportedly so extensive and the regulations so confusing that some victims have been quoted as saying that they don't even believe the SBA intends to lend out the money at its disposal. But, as with so many other aspects of the rebuilding process, many like Mike Yuja found that the process really boils down to how smart you are about it and how persistent.

It turns out, in addition to the requirement about applying through FEMA first, the SBA system has "an even trickier kind of catch-22 you need to figure a way around," says Yuja. The 36-year-old New Orleans medical equipment rep had $180,000 worth of flood insurance, or about half his total losses, making him a classic candidate to have his loan recalled by his mortgage company. Yuja had no problem with that, especially since the main eligibility prerequisite for an SBA loan application in his situation is that you have a "demand letter" from your mortgage company demanding you pay off your loan. The screwball antics began when the check from the insurance company arrived before Chase Mortgage had written its demand letter. "I called Chase and told them

Another, even more insider, IRS provision that may help in a disaster is the sales tax clause. Since 2003 (technically it expired in January 2006, but will likely be extended), everyone has been entitled to choose whether they want to claim a federal deduction for their state income tax payment or the aggregate amount of sales tax they paid that year. For most folks, the income tax is the higher number and the one they'd want to choose. But if you're suddenly re-building a house, the sales tax on all those tens of thousands of dollars in building materials often makes it considerably more attractive to choose option B.

I needed the letter, and that in the meantime I was going to mail them the insurance check so they could endorse it, and then to please mail it back to me so I could deposit it. But they said they wanted me to endorse it and then mail it to them to pay off my mortgage. I tried to explain that if I did that without first getting their letter, I would no longer qualify for the SBA loan. They kept saying, 'Just send us the check.' And I kept saying, 'You don't understand, I need the letter.' I swear, I must have made over 50 phone calls. If I had a desk job, I never would have been able to do it. Finally, I found a woman in a Chase office in Monroe, Louisiana, who said, 'Okay, I'll write you a letter.' I finally got it and mailed it into SBA; then I mailed Chase my check, and now my mortgage is paid off and I have an SBA loan commitment for $234,000 at 2.6 percent that I can use for a new house."

And for the Yujas, that was what would now be considered a very good

"I swear, I must have made 50 phone calls. If I had a desk job, I never would have been able to do it."

day. That's not to say life for this family is anywhere back to normal. Mike figures that they're still about $200,000 in the hole. Dedicated lifelong New Orleans residents, they recently moved to Houston because most of the hospitals Mike serviced in southeastern Louisiana remain closed. His wife, Stacey, a speech pathologist, is having to start building up a new clientele from scratch. Stacey's sister and brother-in-law were hit even harder; her brother-in-law wound up in the hospital with a heart infection after trying to clean out mold from his sporting goods store. Mike's mother's house, where she'd been living with her 89-year-old father, was also destroyed. (Mike's father died just three months before the hurricane.) The Yujas' 4-year-old son was so discombobulated by being uprooted from his favorite toys and friends that, "he cried at his new pre-school every morning for three months straight," says Mike.

"It's definitely been a roller coaster," Mike adds. But like thousands of other American families each year, the Yujas are determined to face forward, with all hands on the safety bar certainly, and keep riding.

It also helps to know that with a paid-off mortgage on a once-prime piece of New Orleans real estate, whose value can only go up from here, plus a loan commitment for $234,000 at 2.6 percent, "things could definitely be worse."

They're survivors, in other words. As Mike says, "What else are you going to do?"

THINGS TO REMEMBER

THINGS TO REMEMBER

CONCLUSION

YOU SHOULD FEEL PROUD of yourself. By rights, you and your family can now consider yourselves some of the most prepared people in America. You have instructions on compiling a stockpile of food, water, and battery-operated lights and radios that will get you through any extended power outage. You have a medical kit checklist drawn up by one of the Homeland Security Department's chief emergency medicine doctors. You know more about insurance and how it relates to disasters than most insurance agents. Your communication plan was designed by the same expert who advises federal agencies. Your home, shelter, and evacuation strategies have been plotted out with all of the latest research and engineering standards in mind. You have advice on navigating a reconstruction project from the most progressive homebuilder's organization in America, and on making up for cash

shortfalls from some of its leading accountants. Perhaps best of all, you have priceless tips, hard lessons, and motivation from families who have been there: the Yujas, Goolsbys, Heberts, Gallodoros, Stices, Kellehers, and Winstons.

If you haven't already, you really should pop the Your Survival™ DVD into your DVD player or use your computer to log onto yoursurvival.com to listen to more of these people's stories. It's impossible to hear their descriptions of hiding in bathrooms under mattresses or of running down sliding hillsides chased by garages with wires exploding all around them without feeling inspired, and a little humbled, by the strength of ordinary people thrust into extraordinary circumstances.

And these families didn't even have the benefit of a website packed with interactive resources at their beck and call 24 hours a day; a 90+ minute DVD of detailed home improvement instructions and more insider tips and demonstrations; or this 160–page preparedness and response guide.

Diane Stevens, a California mother of two, had an interesting comment when asked how her children, then 11 and 15, coped with the trauma of surviving the 2005 Laguna Beach Landslide. "I was actually surprised it didn't affect them more. I think they were young enough that it made them feel like superheroes."

As adults, of course, we all know better than to put our trust in superpowers. But the Your Survival™ Planning, Response, and Recovery Program coupled with the remarkable resilience of the human spirit—now that's a different story.

RECOMMENDED PRODUCTS

For your convenience, we've listed here all of the Recommended Products listed throughout the book.

Medications

Band-Aids®

Betadyne® antiseptic

Lomitil® or Immodium® anti-diarrheal

Neosporin® or Bacitracin® antibacterial ointment

EpiPen® epinephrine dispenser to prevent anaphylactic shock

Ciprofloxacin® prescription antibiotic

Tamiflu®, Relenza® antiviral prescription medications to treat bird flu

Food and Water

55-gallon water drum ($50)

Gatorade® electrolyte drinks

Katadyn™ Hiker water filter ($55)

Sopakco™ Meals, Ready to Eat ($70)

Household Supplies

Rubbermaid® handled 9x9x12 inch plastic tote ($10)

Quake Hold™ putty for securing valuables to shelves ($5)

Gas shut-off wrench ($20)

Maglite® LED flashlight ($35)

Garrity® Rechargeable Flashlight ($24)

Garrity® hurricane lamp ($40)

Big Bang®, Princeton Tectonics® headlamps ($19)

9000 BTU Mr. Heater® "Portable Buddy" portable propane heater ($87.50)

Coleman Powermate Pulse™ portable generator ($480)

Coleman®, Generac®, Onan® standby generators ($2,500-$4,000)

Communications Equipment

Radio Shack® GMRS/FRS walkie-talkie ($25)

Iridium®, Globalstar® sat phones (reconditioned, $400)

HOT LINKS

For your convenience, we've listed here all of the Hot Links listed throughout the book.

Identifying Your Risks

USC Database

www.cas.sc.edu/geog/hrl/SHELDUS.html

See disasters that have occurred in your county.

Chemical Scorecard

scorecard.org/env-releases/

See chemical facilities in your area.

Firewise Plant List

www.firewise.org/usa/fw_plantlists.html

See what plants are fire-resistant.

The Weather Channel

www.weather.com/maps/news/septnonactive/

atlanticoceansatellite_large_animated.html

Track hurricanes and other storms.

National Oceanic and Atmospheric Administrations National Weather Service

www.nws.noaa.gov/radar_tab.php

Track tornadoes and other storms.

Preparing for Disasters

Know Your Stuff

www.knowyourstuff.org/download.htm

Download free home-inventorying software.

Captain Dave's Survival Shop

captaindaves.com/shop/water.html

Stock up on water and other survival supplies, like MREs.

American Institute of Certified Public Accountants
Personal Financial Planning Center

www.aicpa.org/CredentialsRefWeb/PFSCredentialSearchPage.aspx

Find an accountant to get your finances in order.

Getting Help After the Crisis

Red Cross Chapters

www.redcross.org/where/chapts.asp

Find your local Red Cross chapter.

Red Cross Partners

www.redcross.org/news/ds/hurricanes/2005/gethelp.html#financial

Find other organizations that can help.

National Mental Health Association Database

www.nmha.org/go/searchMHA

Find a therapist who can help you cope.

Federal Emergency Management Agency Application Form

www.fema.gov/assistance/index.shtm

Apply for financial assistance from FEMA.

FEMA Partners

www.disasteraid.fema.gov/IAC/DataView.do?page=disasters

Find other government agencies that can help.

Below-Market Temporary Housing

rims.fema.gov/hportal/home.htm

Find below market temporary housing.

Habitat for Humanity

www.habitat.org/getinv/apply.aspx

Apply for a Habitat for Humanity home.

Extreme Makeover: Home Edition

abc.go.com/primetime/xtremehome/casting.html

Apply to be on Extreme Makeover: Home Edition.

CHECKLISTS

For your convenience, we've pulled together here all of the checklists and lists of questions from throughout the book.

SEVEN QUESTIONS ABOUT YOUR PROPERTY

1. How high does the house sit in relation to the surrounding terrain? Put another way, if your neighborhood was to flood would your house be one of the first or last underwater?

2. Do you know where the dams or dykes are in your area, and what kind of shape they're in?

3. How close is your house to dense brush or other flammable areas?

4. Does it sit on a steep slope that could be prone to landslides?

_____

_____

_____

_____

5. What's the ground underneath the house like? Is it made of bedrock and dense soils that could help absorb the impact of an earthquake, or loose fill that could "liquefy" and open like a giant mouth and swallow up everything you own?

_____

_____

_____

_____

6. How close are you to a nuclear power plant or toxic chemical production or storage facilities?

_____

_____

_____

_____

7. Is the property located near one of the high-profile cities or tourist attractions thought to be likely terrorist targets?

_____

_____

_____

_____

EIGHT QUESTIONS FOR YOUR INSURANCE AGENT

1. "Will my policy pay for the guaranteed replacement cost or just the replacement cost of damages to my house?"

_____

_____

_____

_____

_____

2. "What kind of contents coverage do I have?"

_____

_____

_____

_____

3. "Do I need flood insurance?"

_____

_____

_____

_____

4. "Do I need more flood insurance?"

_____

_____

_____

_____

_____

5. "What about earthquake or mudslide insurance?"

_____

_____

_____

_____

_____

6. "Are there any other specific provisions I should consider?"

_____

_____

_____

_____

_____

7. "How much is all this going to cost?"

_____

_____

_____

_____

_____

8. "So bottom line: Do I have enough?"

_____

_____

_____

_____

_____

SAMPLE DISASTER GROCERY LIST
FOR THE TYPICAL FAMILY OF FOUR

✓ 16 cans tuna, salmon, and/or sardines
✓ 12 cans chicken
✓ 4 cans chili
✓ 4 cans baked beans
✓ 4 cans other beans
✓ 12 cans soups and stews
✓ 16 cans fruit
✓ 6 boxes pasta
✓ 1 large bag rice
✓ 1 jar pickles
✓ 1 16-oz bottle cooking oil
✓ 3 cartons granola, breakfast or power bars
✓ 2 bags dried fruit
✓ 2 40-oz jars peanut butter
✓ 2 jars jelly
✓ 4 boxes crackers
✓ 3 gallons powdered milk

✓ 1 can coffee
✓ 2 boxes oatmeal
✓ 6 boxes dried cereal
✓ 2 boxes pancake mix
✓ 8 rolls paper towels
✓ 7 boxes garbage bags
✓ 2 cans dried nuts
✓ 1 package each paper plates, bowls, cups, utensils
✓ 12 rolls toilet paper
✓ 2 bottles hand sanitizer
✓ Tube toothpaste, toothbrushes, soap, large bottle, shampoo
✓ 1 large bag dried pet food and cat litter (for families with pets)
✓ Matches
✓ Whistle
✓ Playing cards, board games

DR. SUSAN BRIGGS'
ULTIMATE DISASTER EMERGENCY MEDICINE KIT

✔ A laminated list of every family member's allergies, chronic medical conditions, and prescriptions, including dosages, plus a week's worth of spare doses for each medication

✔ An official "yellow card" vaccination record for each family member, available from most doctor's offices or any travel medicine clinic. Simply call your physician for help in filling them out. Each card should include the current status of everyone's shots. Anyone not up to date on tetanus should get a booster, and anyone with special skills who might be called on as a first responder should consider getting vaccinated for hepatitis A and B.

✔ A prescription for Ciprofloxacin®, usually available from your doctor. The most common risk for infection in a disaster is common traveler's-type diarrhea from waterborne bacteria, and Cipro is the best antibiotic for knocking it out.

✔ Two 8 oz. bottles of electrolyte drinks, like Gatorade® brand

✔ Small packages or bottles of anti-diarrheals (Lomotil® or Imodium®), antacids, antihistamine, acetaminophen, and ibuprofen

✔ EpiPen®, injector to prevent anaphylactic shock in the event of a severe allergic reaction

✔ An assortment of bandages, including two dozen Band-Aids® brand bandages, a half dozen sterile gauze pads, one conforming gauze roll, one Ace® brand wrap, and one roll of 2-inch adhesive tape

✔ Betadyne® anticeptic, a box of antiseptic wipes and germicidal hand wipes, a tube of anti-bacterial ointment (Neosporin® or Bacitracin® brand), and two pairs of non-sterile latex gloves

✔ Cold pack

✔ Small scissors, tweezers, and a thermometer

✔ Generic soft water-resistant backpack, for easy transport in a "bug-out" situation (see page 36)

SAMPLE BUG-OUT BAG

✓ A change of durable clothes suitable for layering (T-shirt, flannel shirt, etc.), including season-appropriate jacket and other outerwear

✓ A pair of comfortable already broken-in shoes

✓ A couple of extra pairs of socks and underwear

✓ Quart of water

✓ Handful of healthy snacks and energy bars

✓ Spare glasses or contact lenses and solution

✓ Personal toiletries

✓ Stuffed animal

✓ Deck of cards

MAINTENENCE CHECKLIST

Once every few years:

✓ Review publicly available disaster sources like flood maps and the county disaster and chemical facility registries.

Once a year:

✓ Check the condition of your roof.

✓ Change batteries in flashlights, lamps, and radios, and replace spares with a fresh batch.

✓ Review and possibly raise limits on insurance policies (unless you have guaranteed replacement cost coverage).

✓ Replace all prescription and over-the-counter medications in your emergency medicine kit.

✓ Replace food and water in vehicle bug-out box.

Once every six months:

✓ Rotate food in disaster supply into everyday cabinets and replace with fresh batch.

Once a season:

✓ Change clothes in bug-out bags to more season-appropriate attire.

✓ Test to make sure your sump pump is operating properly.

GLOSSARY

ADJUSTOR The person assigned by an insurance company to handle a claim and determine the reimbursement amount. After a major loss, like that associated with a disaster, he or she will often personally inspect the damages to the home, calculating the settlement based upon certain pre-set formulas.

AMENDED TAX RETURN A supplemental tax return filed after the standard April 15 deadline, frequently in connection with a major disaster. In filing such a claim, qualified victims can deduct their un-reimbursed property damages from the previous years' taxable income. The combined refund can run into the tens of thousands of dollars.

BUG-OUT BAG A backpack or other similar container packed with a personal supply of essential equipment, such as a change of clothes, snacks, water, and flashlight, to be used in the event of an evacuation.

CASH VALUE One of two formulas used by insurance companies to reimburse policy-holders for the damaged contents of a home. In contrast to the other formula (known as "replacement value contents coverage") that pays to replace possessions with the same items, cash value only reimburses the policyholder for the original purchase price of the items less depreciation.

CONTAINMENT ROOM Any room sealed off from inside by plastic sheeting and duct tape to protect the inhabitants from a chemical, biological, or nuclear hazard.

DEFENSIBLE SPACE The strip of grass, perennials, pavers, and other non-flammable materials surrounding a home serving as a protective barrier against wildfires.

DEMAND LETTER A legal document issued by a mortgage company requiring a lender to pay off the mortgage on a property. Often comes into play when an underinsured home has been destroyed, thereby substantially reducing the collateral backing up the loan.

FLOOD INSURANCE The only insurance that pays for property damage from flooding. Available through regular insurance providers from the federal flood insurance program, the standard flood insurance policy can cost anywhere from $300 to $1,000 for up to $250,000 in coverage.

HURRICANE SHUTTERS Sturdy sheets of plywood, metal, or plexiglass fitted over windows to help seal off the interior of a house from the high winds associated with hurricanes.

HURRICANE CLIPS Simple 3-inch metal plates nailed into the corner of joists to increase the stability of a roof when exposed to hurricane-force winds.

ICE (IN CASE OF EMERGENCY) An acronym that emergency personnel increasingly recommend people punch into their cell phones along with the number of the person they'd want contacted if they're injured and can't respond.

LED Stands for "light-emitting diode," and refers to a type of energy-efficient bulb that greatly extends the life of flashlight batteries.

MEALS READY TO EAT Commonly known by its acronym, MREs, these lightweight hermetically sealed rations were originally developed by the U.S. military for use in the battlefield, but also make for a convenient—and surprisingly palatable—source of food during a disaster evacuation.

NOAA® WEATHER RADIO A radio with a special signal operated by the National Weather Service branch of the National Oceanographic and

Atmospheric Agency that alerts users to the presence of severe weather in their areas. Especially popular in tornado-prone portions of the Southwest, where the early warning can be a lifesaver.

PUBLIC ADJUSTOR Like an adjustor, except the person is hired by the policyholder to contest the reimbursement amount offered by the insurance company. Public adjustors usually charge a flat fee of around $300.

REPLACEMENT COST The slightly misleading term used by the insurance industry to describe the property coverage in the most common type of homeowner's policy. Replacement cost coverage does not pay to replace or fix a home severely damaged by disaster—it only does so up to certain pre-set limits in the policy, usually tied to homebuilding costs at the time the policy was written. Just to add to the confusion, replacement cost contents coverage (see "cash value," on the previous page) does pay to replace the possessions inside the home with the same items.

SBA LOAN A low-interest loan for business owners available from the Small Business Administration available to qualified underinsured disaster victims.

SAFE ROOM A shelter built inside a home to precise specifications that will withstand the impact of a severe tornado.

SHUT-OFF WRENCH A type of nonadjustable wrench with a standardized narrow rectangular opening that's sized to fit the shut-off valve on the gas main inside a dwelling. Found at most hardware stores, it's especially recommended in areas at risk for tornados and earthquakes, both of which can rupture gas lines.

STANDBY SYSTEM The most advanced form of private generator, hardwired directly into a house's electrical system and powered by the local municipality's gas or propane lines.

"STORM TROOPER" The nickname given adjustors flown in by insurance companies from other states to work the aftermath of a major disaster.

TORNADO ALLEY The region, encompassing North Texas, Oklahoma, and Kansas, at greatest risk in the United States for tornados.

2X3 DISH A new, larger type of roof dish offered by satellite TV providers. Because it bypasses ground relay stations and beams its signals directly up to satellites, it's one of the most disaster-proof forms of communication on the market. A 2x3 dish, well-charged laptop, and Internet service from a satellite TV provider would theoretically remain operational through even the worst disaster.

WARNING The higher of two alerts issued by forecasters and local authorities advising residents of an impending hazard. Translation: Whatever severe event has been predicted is definitely on its way.

WATCH The first-level alert issued by forecasters and authorities, meaning: just be aware of the possibility of a hazard and stay tuned to additional developments.

WIND RATING The criteria used to judge the ability of building materials such as roof shingles to stand up to high winds. The highest rating is H, awarded to products that take winds of up to 140 miles an hour.

YELLOW CARD A pocket-sized yellow-colored document available from most doctor's offices or any travel medicine clinic listing the holder's vaccination record. Recommended in a disaster situation so medical personnel can quickly determine the person's status for tetanus or other vaccines that might be necessitated by unsanitary conditions.

DISASTER SEVERITY RATING SCALES

HURRICANES
SAFFIR SIMPSON SCALE

When we talk about a "Category 3" or "Cat 4" hurricane we're referring to this 1-5 scale, developed in 1969 by civil engineer Herbert Saffir and National Hurricane Center director Bob Simpson. Saffir had been commissioned by the United Nations to study the damage to low-cost housing in hurricane-prone areas. Realizing the need for a standard rating system like what already existed at the time for earthquakes, he came up with five different categories based on wind speed, and then turned to Simpson to add in the effects of flooding.

CATEGORY	WINDS (mph)	TYPICAL STORM SURGE
1	74-95	4'-5'
2	96-110	6'-8'
3	111-130	9'-12'
4	131-155	13'-18'
5	≥155	≥18'

TORNADOES
FUJITA SCALE

Legendary University of Chicago meteorologist Tetsuya "Ted" Fujita developed this 1-5 scale in 1971 in collaboration with Allen Pearson, then head of the National Severe Storms Forecast Center. (It's also sometimes known as the Fujita-Pearson Scale.) Because of the difficulty in gauging wind speed inside a tornado, the scale is based as much on Fujita's subjective-sounding descriptions of the damage as it is on actual measurements. In fact, starting in February 2007, the scale was officially superseded in the U.S. by a slightly more precise 1-5 system known as the Enhanced Fujita Scale. The distinctions are mostly technical, though, and "F4" or "F5" still remain a more common way to refer to a cataclysmic tornado than "EF4" or "EF5."

CATEGORY	WINDS (mph)	TYPICAL DAMAGE
F0	< 73	Light. Some damage to chimneys; branches broken off trees; shallow-rooted trees pushed over; sign boards damaged.
F1	73-112	Moderate. The lower limit is the beginning of hurricane wind speed; peels surface off roots; mobile homes pushed off foundations or overturned; moving autos pushed off the roads; attached garages may be destroyed.
F2	113-157	Considerable. Roofs torn off frame houses; mobile homes demolished; boxcars overturned; large trees snapped or uprooted; light-object missiles generated.
F3	158-206	Severe. Roofs and some walls torn off well-constructed houses; trains overturned; most trees in forest uprooted; heavy cars lifted off ground and thrown.
F4	207-260	Devastating. Well-constructed homes leveled; structures with weak foundations blown away some distance; cars thrown and large missiles generated.
F5	261-318	Incredible. Strong frame houses lifted off foundations and carried considerable distances to disintegrate; automobile-sized missiles fly through the air in excess of 100 yards; trees debarked; steel reinforced concrete structures badly damaged; incredible phenomena will occur.

EARTHQUAKES
RICHTER MAGNITUDE SCALE

The most technically complicated of the disaster rating systems, the Richter Scale was originally developed in 1935 by California Institute of Technology seismologist Charles Richter as part of a research project. The scale is based on the measurements taken by an instrument known as a seismometer. When an earthquake occurs, energy is released underground that's detected by the seismometer and recorded as waves on a graph. A mathematical equation is then used to translate the height of those waves into a single number on a 1-10 scale.

DESCRIPTION	RICHTER MAGNITUDE	EARTHQUAKE EFFECTS
Micro	<2.0	Not felt.
Very Minor	2.0-2.9	Generally felt.
Minor	3.0-3.9	Often felt, but rarely causes damage.
Light	4.0-4.9	Noticeable shaking of indoor items, rattling noises, significant damage unlikely.
Moderate	5.0-5.9	Can cause major damage to poorly constructed buildings over small regions. At most slight damage to well-designed buildings.
Strong	6.0-6.9	Can be destructive in areas up to about 100 miles across in populated areas.

DESCRIPTION (CONT'D)	RICHTER MAGNITUDE (CONT'D)	EARTHQUAKE EFFECTS (CONT'D)
Major	7.0-7.9	Can cause serious damage over even larger areas.
Great	8.0-8.9	Can cause serious damage in areas several hundred miles across.
Rare Great	9.0-9.9	Devastating in areas several thousand miles across.
Meteroric	10.0-?	Never recorded.

PANDEMICS

PANDEMIC SEVERITY INDEX

This little-known scale was just recently adopted by the federal government in February 2007 as part of its avian influenza pandemic preparedness planning efforts. It's purely based on the percentage of infected patients who die from a disease outbreak, otherwise known as the infectious agent's "Case-Fatality Ratio." As an example, the influenza pandemics of 1957 and 1968 both would have been Category 2 pandemics, while the severe 1918-19 Spanish Flu would have been a Category 5.

CATEGORY	CASE-FATALITY RATIO
1	<0.1%
2	0.1-0.5%
3	.5-1.0%
4	1.0-2.0%
5	>2.0%

SOME OF THE WORST DISASTERS IN U.S. HISTORY

"BILLION-DOLLAR" TORNADO America's costliest tornado. Registering wind speeds of 318 miles per hour, it ripped through Moore, Oklahoma City, and surrounding communities on the evening of May 3, 1999, killing 36 and destroying more than 8,000 buildings and 2,000 homes.

BLIZZARD OF 1888 A three-day blizzard in mid-March 1888 that buried the Northeast under four feet of snow and drifts as high as 40 feet. New York, Boston, Philadelphia, and Washington, D.C., were all cut off for days, and 400 people were killed.

GALVESTON HURRICANE Before Katrina this 1900 storm was considered America's worst hurricane, and is still its deadliest. At the time the hurricane washed ashore with a 15-foot storm surge the highest point on Galveston Island, TX, was only 8.7 feet. More than 8,000 Galvestonians died.

GREAT MISSISSIPPI FLOOD On May 6, 1927 the Mississippi River broke from its levee system in 145 different locations, flooding 27,00 square miles, including parts of Illinois, Kentucky, Louisiana, Mississippi, Tennessee, and 13 percent of the state of Arkansas. Official death toll was 247, though some estimates put it as high as 1,000.

GREAT MIDWEST FLOOD With $20 billion in damages this May 1993 catastrophe was America's costliest flood until Katrina. The product of record rainfall that caused hundreds of levee breaches along the Mississippi and Missouri rivers, the flooding inundated portions of nine states.

HURRICANE KATRINA Now the benchmark for U.S. hurricanes. The September 2005 storm slammed into the Gulf Coast with a 14-foot storm surge that obliterated waterfront communities and overwhelmed the levees of

New Orleans. Total tab: $81.5 billion, and a once-great city reduced to half its former size.

HURRICANE ANDREW The hurricane that changed the culture of disaster preparedness in Florida. One of only three Category 5 hurricanes to make landfall in the U.S. over the past 100 years, it flattened homes throughout the Miami area, but particularly poorly constructed new construction in Homestead. All told damages exceeded $26 billion.

JOHNSTOWN FLOOD When the earthen South Fork Dam burst on May 31, 1889, a wall of water 100 feet high smashed into Johnston, PA, at 40 miles per hour, destroying much of the town and drowning 2,200.

MOUNT ST. HELENS VOLCANO The volcano's eruption on May 18, 1980 leveled forests, buildings, and highways over 230 square miles.

NORTHRIDGE EARTHQUAKE Although the quake that struck Los Angeles at 4:30 A.M. January 17, 1994, registered "only" a moderate 6.7 on the Richter scale, other seismic factors helped make it America's most destructive since the 1906 San Francisco earthquake. Its $25.7 billion tab also made it the country's most expensive natural disaster before Katrina.

PESHTIGO FIRE The nation's worst wildfire, this October 1871 blaze in northeastern Wisconsin burned more than 3.8 million acres, completely destroyed nine towns, and killed 1,500.

SAN FRANCISCO EARTHQUAKE The model for "the Big One" that is the basis for much of California's earthquake planning. Occurring in the early morning hours of April 18, 1906, it registered between 7.7 and 8.3 on the Richter scale and touched off fires that torched four square miles. Experts estimate its death toll of 470 would exceed 3,000 if a similar quake struck today.

"STORM OF THE CENTURY" The worst winter storm of the 20th century. The massive blizzard that blanketed the Eastern U.S. from March 12-15, 1993, caused 300 deaths, an estimated $10 billion in damages, and left much of the Southeast without power for up to 10 days.

SEPTEMBER 11 Rarely has a disaster concentrated on such a small area affected so many so profoundly. Although the direct economic impact of the 2001 terrorist attacks was more limited than originally believed, the cost of clean-up and insured losses still likely topped $100 billion, greater even than Katrina. And, of course, that's not counting the impact on foreign policy, domestic security, indeed, the whole way most Americans view the world.

SPANISH FLU The most destructive pandemic in human history and by far the deadliest natural disaster on American shores. When today's health officials speculate on the possible effects of an avian flu pandemic, they use this 1918 outbreak of an unusually severe strain of Influenza A as the model for the worst-case scenario. More than 100 million died worldwide in just 18 months, 500,000-675,000 of them in the U.S. Even in communities where mortality was relatively low, so many were infected that much of everyday life ground to a halt for weeks.

"TRI-STATE TORNADO" Still the deadliest tornado on record, it killed more than 690 people in Missouri, Illinois, and Indiana, and caused $25 million in property damage in 1925 dollars.

INDEX